Garbage In, Garbage Out

Garbage In,

Garbage Out

Solving the Problems with
Long-Distance Trash Transport

VIVIAN E. THOMSON

University of Virginia Press   *Charlottesville and London*

University of Virginia Press
© 2009 by the Rector and Visitors of the University of Virginia
All rights reserved
Printed in the United States of America on acid-free paper

First published 2009

9 8 7 6 5 4 3 2 1

Library of Congress Cataloging-in-Publication Data
Thomson, Vivian E., 1956–
Garbage in, garbage out : solving the problems with long-distance trash transport / Vivian E.
Thomson.
p. cm.
Includes bibliographical references and index.
ISBN 978-0-8139-2824-1 (cloth : alk. paper) — ISBN 978-0-8139-2825-8 (pbk. : alk. paper)
ISBN 978-0-8139-2871-5 (e-book)
1. Refuse and refuse disposal—United States—Management. 2. Refuse and refuse disposal—
Transportation—United States. 3. Refuse and refuse disposal—Government policy—United
States. 4. Waste disposal sites—United States—Management. 5. Interstate commerce—
United States. I. Title.
TD788.T56 2009
363.72′85560973—dc22
2009005844

Contents

Illustrations

Acknowledgments

A theme lying just below the surface of this book is that everything is connected to everything else. In similar fashion, while conducting research for and writing this book, I was dependent on the work and special skills of many professionals. To them I owe my first thanks.

Jim McCarthy of the Congressional Research Service has written several methodical reports that are the most reputable source of summary statistics on interstate trash transport. Without Jim's thorough analyses this book could not have been written. He also offered help and advice on numerous occasions. Jim is the model public servant; his expertise is second to none. Bob Burnley, Director of the Virginia Department of Environmental Quality from 2002 to 2006, provided invaluable insights and information, drawing upon his decades of experience with environmental issues in the Commonwealth. Karen Sismour, Director of the Waste Division at the Virginia Department of Environmental Quality, and her staff, always responded quickly to my repeated requests for information, despite the many demands on their time. Other DEQ staff who provided helpful information include Leslie Beckwith, Debra Miller, Tom Modena, and Sanjay Thirunagari. Davis Walsh, legislative assistant to Virginia senator Creigh Deeds, helped untangle the somewhat complicated history of one legislative proposal's fate.

Dan Shean is a shining star in the firmament of my former students. His first independent work as a second-year undergraduate at the University of Virginia was a summer of research on the movement of trash between New York State and Virginia. In this work, as in all of his subsequent coursework for me, Dan evinced a quiet brilliance, discipline, and dedication to environmental policy. He wrote a paper on trash transport in his third year at the University of Virginia School of Law, and I am indebted to him for the ideas and research described in that work. This book is inestimably better because of our six years' worth of interaction as professor and student.

Itaru Okuda translated Japanese documents that were unavailable in English and worked patiently with me during the two years he spent as a guest scholar at the University of Virginia. That association culminated in a joint paper on the regionalization of municipal solid waste (MSW) management in Japan. It is because of Dr. Okuda that the comparative analysis in this book includes information on Japan; he also supplied photos of Tokyo's incinerators and neatly arranged recycling bags. Dr. Okuda is one of the most intellectually curious, impeccable researchers I have met, and I count myself lucky to be among his professional colleagues.

In Belgium, Rudy Meeus, director of the waste agency in Flanders, and his top aide, Phillipe Van de Velde, took time to educate me in the ways of Flemish MSW management. The Flemish are among the leaders in implementing the European Union's intertwined principles of precaution, self-sufficiency, pollution prevention, proximity, and polluter pays; as a result, we have much to learn from them. I am also indebted generally to the Danes. While a Fulbright Professor in Denmark in 2001-2, I came to appreciate the Danes' determined dedication to waste prevention, which flows from their technical sophistication and long-held devotion to the public good.

Representatives of European industry groups, NGOs, and government institutions helped me understand the European Union's approach to MSW management. Julian Carroll of EuroPen, Jacques Hoffenberg of Waste Denmark, and Nathalie Cliquot of the European Environment Bureau shared their valuable perspectives in personal interviews. Karin Jordon of Eurostat helped clarify the European Union's waste data.

Chris Gist, a GIS specialist in the Scholars' Lab at the University of Virginia's Alderman Library, painstakingly assembled the maps of landfills in Virginia. Shelly Schneider of Franklin Associates provided analytical assistance at several points during my research. Mike Giuranna of the U.S. Environmental Protection Agency provided timely and useful information.

While I am immensely grateful to these individuals for their assistance, I take full responsibility for the contents of this book. All observations and opinions are mine and should not be construed to represent those of any other individual or organization.

While this book was in progress, I served as vice-chair of the Virginia Air Pollution Control Board. Between 2006 and 2008 the board confronted some especially controversial, time-consuming issues. I am grateful to my fellow board members for their understanding concerning my publishing deadlines. Board members Hullie Moore and Bruce Buckheit, my like-minded partners in many board-related actions, persevered in the face of seemingly insurmountable obstacles in order to serve the public good. By their example they inspired me to pursue the same goals with this book.

The University of Virginia's Department of Environmental Sciences provided travel funds, as did the University's Small Grants Program. *Environmental Management*'s editor permitted me to use material appearing in that journal.

The editorial staff at the University of Virginia Press are impressive for their professionalism, skill, and responsiveness to my questions. Penny Kaiserlian is not only a masterly, seasoned editor, she is clear and kind, and she understands well the art of communicating constructive criticism. Ruth Steinberg, Ellen Satrom and Angie Hogan patiently walked me through the manuscript preparation process and provided encouragement at key junctures.

My second set of thanks is personal. My sister, Jean Thomson Black, Executive Science Editor at Yale University Press, always made herself available to provide helpful feedback and support. I knew I could trust her guidance. My parents, Jim and Selma, held me to the highest standards and encouraged the life of the mind. From my mother and her mother, Flora, I first learned about taking care of things, reusing things instead of discarding them, conserving resources, and living modestly but well. My mother showed me in her life's work that women can and should assume important positions of leadership in the professional world. My daughters, Amelia and Flora, seem inclined to carry on this tradition of high aspirations. I am prouder of them than I can say. In their work they embody all of my best principles about challenging one's intellect and living a good, socially conscious life.

Harry Potter was my devoted canine companion from start to finish. He never left my side and always gave quiet, undemanding comfort.

My husband, Pat Roach, has inspired me in countless ways. From the beginning of our courtship we argued about trash, and from those debates grew a much stronger book than it would otherwise have been. He is insatiably curious, and his questions forced me to explore new angles. He is a skillful writer whose editorial comments have made the book clearer. He has been patient on the many weekends when I had to work. He has read the book from start to finish. When I had to meet a critical publishing deadline in the middle of a frantically busy semester, Pat converted the book's entire set of citations from the author-date system to endnotes and bibliography format. I am definitely the lucky one.

Garbage In, Garbage Out

Everything Is Trash

Trash is an inherently contradictory material. On the one hand, it has attractive qualities, at least for some of us. Archaeologists delight in garbage because the cast-off things of peoples long gone tell us about how they lived and died. Kids and dogs paw through trash looking for fun, interesting, useful items, and discarded papers or photos can be a treasure trove of historical information.

But trash is more than a potential fount of information: it is a fundamental indicator of life. Much as the acrid, black smoke emanating from industrial smokestacks used to mean that business was good, the existence of garbage shows that life is present. Even as we discover beneficial uses for waste—for example, as "food" for other processes—that does not change the fundamental fact that we cannot function without making some waste.[1]

On the other hand, we want to be rid of trash because it is messy and because some of its components are hazardous to human health and to other living organisms. Granted, we often store unwanted items that are not quite trash yet. Everyone's basement, attic, or closets hold items that

Everyone's basement, attic, or closets hold items that are in limbo. (© Zits Partnership. King Features Syndicate)

are in limbo, especially formerly valuable items, like used electronics, that we might reuse or recycle. Eventually we find a repository even for long-stored items, by consigning them to a yard sale, garbage can, recycling bin, or compost heap.

As one trash hauler summed things up, "Everything is trash." By this he meant that all materials and all living things, no matter how valuable, eventually die, deteriorate, or become obsolete. And then they must be removed to somewhere else where they can be buried, burned, reused, or recycled.[2]

This same incongruity runs through policy debates on whether to regulate the interstate transport of trash: Is trash to be regarded first and foremost as something of value? Or, alternatively, as pollution? To waste management firms and to the many communities that host and reap tax benefits from waste facilities, trash is valuable commerce. The Supreme Court has reinforced in several decisions its view that trash transport is commerce and that, therefore, states may not impede the interstate movement of trash unless Congress allows them to do so.

However, even if garbage is commerce in the Supreme Court's eyes, it is also pollution. Although modern waste facilities must meet much more stringent health and environmental standards than the town dumps they replaced, they are still sources of air and water contaminants. In the United States, landfills are the largest source of human-generated methane—a powerful greenhouse gas—and carcinogens like benzene and vinyl chloride are among the exotic cocktail of trace gases that emanate from them. Landfill leachate often contains toxic compounds, and despite elaborate modern precautionary measures which include soil covers, synthetic liners, and leachate collection systems, landfills can contaminate groundwater or nearby surface waters. In fact, the United States Environmental Protection Agency has concluded that all landfills will eventually leak liquids into the surrounding environment. Municipal waste incinerators, sometimes erroneously thought to be an alternative to landfills, transform trash into heat and ash, and create an air pollution stream that contains harmful compounds like fine particulate matter, mercury, dioxin, and nitrogen oxides, that must be controlled as directed by national and state regulations. Incinerator ash from the burning of municipal solid waste must be reused or sent to a landfill.[3]

Trash's paradoxical status as both pollution and commerce is thrown into relief when we examine the issue of long-distance transport within the United States. Garbage has long been trucked, barged, and moved by rail across state lines, but such interstate movement has increased noticeably in the past fifteen years. In 2005, 25 percent of disposed or incinerated municipal solid waste, or MSW (the technical term for trash), traveled to another state, which represents an increase of 147 percent in ten years.[4] This increase is due in part to stricter environmental regulations that have caused many old, local landfills to shut down. So the dramatic increase in commercial trash transport, created in part by new environmental rules, has in turn sparked criticisms on the environmental grounds that more communities are not only dumping their trash in someone else's back yard, they are transporting that trash even farther than before.

My home state of Virginia plays a central role in this narrative because in the late 1990s Virginia earned a new, dubious distinction as the second-largest importer of trash in the United States, trailing only its northern neighbor, the state of Pennsylvania. Pennsylvania and Virginia remain in first and second place, respectively, in the rankings of trash-importing states.[5]

Virginians would undoubtedly prefer that outsiders associate their state with its enormously varied natural beauty, which includes spectacular mountain ranges and the Chesapeake Bay, the largest estuary in the United States. But the fact remains that waste management firms have carved huge holes in the ground to dispose of garbage generated in faraway places. Those "mega-landfills" are concentrated in Virginia's

BFI landfill in King and Queen County, Virginia. (Photo courtesy of Virginia Department of Environmental Quality)

Coastal Plain and Piedmont regions. Virginia and Pennsylvania are not alone in this regard. Imported trash has become big business in many other states as well, including Illinois, Indiana, Michigan, and Ohio, which provide final resting places for garbage from New York, New Jersey, Maryland, North Carolina, the District of Columbia, and Canada.

In an emblematic trash transport case that attracted attention from the major news media, the garbage barge *Mobro* left Long Island in March 1987 seeking a dumping ground for its cargo. The *Mobro* traveled up and down the Atlantic Coast, only to return to Long Island two months later, having been refused port at docks in North Carolina, several other southern states, Mexico, and Belize. Once back in Long Island, the barge baked in the summer sun for several weeks while government authorities argued over the fate of its putrescent cargo. Eventually, the *Mobro*'s load came full circle: it was burned in a Brooklyn incinerator and the ash was buried in Islip, Long Island, where the trash had originated.[6]

Since the *Mobro*'s saga, the national press has covered garbage transport issues only sporadically. In the late 1990s, the *Washington Post* and *New York Times* published articles on ill-fated attempts by Governor Gilmore and the Virginia General Assembly to block out-of-state garbage, much of it originating in New York City, from reaching Virginia landfills. And in 2007, American Public Media's radio program *Marketplace* covered trash transport as part of a larger series on consumerism in America.[7]

These occasional bursts of national media attention have not spurred widespread concern over the increase in interstate garbage transport. But some members of Congress have continued to worry about its political and environmental consequences and they have kept it on the national political agenda. Since the early 1990s Congress has entertained, but has never enacted, bills that would allow the states to constrain the movement of garbage from other states. In this book, I describe these legislative proposals and I question whether they address our most critical garbage-related problems.

RATIONALE FOR A BOOK ON TRASH TRANSPORT

In the early twenty-first century the most highly visible environmental problems, like climate change, biodiversity loss, and tropical deforestation, are global in scale. Two recent high-profile books provide laundry lists of the worst environmental problems facing us: habitat destruction; fisheries depletion; genetic diversity loss; soil erosion; species extinction; skyrocketing energy use; contaminated or insufficient drinking water; toxic chemicals; invasive species; climate change; and population growth.[8] In these and similar catalogues of pressing environmental policy issues, garbage and garbage transport tend not to be first on anyone's list.

I do not seek to upend the conventional wisdom by claiming that garbage deserves a starring role in the cast of environmental problems. Rather, I claim that the reason to study garbage transport is that it throws into especially vivid relief the interconnections between the environment, politics, markets, race, and class. While virtually all forms of pollution travel, most forms move in accordance with natural forces like atmospheric winds or water currents.

In contrast, the movement of garbage is under our control. In studying its transport, we must necessarily examine the exercise of economic and political power, and we must also confront questions about consumption levels in America. A book on garbage transport offers the opportunity to move beyond the narrow question of whether we are adequately controlling environmental impacts to much broader questions about how much trash we generate, who gets to regulate it, and who must tolerate its dumping grounds.

OUTLINE OF THE BOOK

Chapter 1 explores the environmental, economic, political, and judicial factors that have landed trash transport on Congress's agenda. I describe the pollution problems associated with trash, which might seem innocuous by comparison with other forms of waste but which present current and future risks in the form of land, air, and water pollution. Chapter 1 sets forth the interlocking roles of federal, state, and local governments in trash management, it discusses regulatory controls for garbage landfills and incinerators, and it describes the trend toward municipal waste management privatization. In chapter 1 I also mention the links between socioeconomic factors and the location of trash management facilities. The Constitution's "dormant Commerce Clause" is introduced, as is its role in garbage transport debates and court decisions.

Legislative proposals to date implicitly assume that the problem to be solved is waste transport across state or local government borders. However, one might argue that our primary problem with waste is that we make too much of it. In chapter 2 I explore whether Americans are wasteful by comparison with the Japanese and with Europeans. The first part of this chapter is theoretical and describes the literature connecting economic growth with pollution. This discussion sets the stage for an empirical analysis, conducted with Dr. Itaru Okuda, in which MSW generation and recycling figures for the United States, the European Union, and Japan are compared. I standardize MSW generation figures across countries so that international comparisons are valid. I also describe historical and projected trends in MSW generation rates. I conclude that Americans generate more MSW per capita than their industrialized nation counterparts. Depending on which statistics are used, MSW generation per unit of economic productivity in the United States is either average or quite high relative to other affluent nations.

I conclude chapter 2 by examining the forces underlying the cross-national differences illuminated in the first part of the chapter. I show that Americans consume more and save less than citizens in the affluent EU-15 and Japan. Then I describe the ways in which policymakers in Japan and in the European Union have embraced the waste management principles of proximity, self-sufficiency, pollution prevention, producer responsibility, and precaution. Those regulatory choices reflect social and cultural norms that have driven the EU Member States and Japan to pursue related goals: to reduce to a minimum the amount of trash sent to landfills, to produce less garbage overall, and to avoid sending trash for disposal to other regions. The proximity principle holds that waste disposal should be as close as possible to home on the grounds that it is wrong to dump trash in someone else's back yard. This is a central organizing idea in the European Union's waste directives and waste shipment regulations, and in Japan's MSW management system as well. No parallel notion animates waste disposal at the state or national level in the United States, although flow control ordinances enacted by many local governments aim to keep trash close to home.

Chapter 3 explores the ways in which environmental justice considerations factor into the trash transport policy arena. I give some background on the environmental justice literature and its claims of unfair distribution of environmental risk. Then I examine the empirical basis for claims that MSW facilities in particular are disproportionately located in minority and/or low-income areas. A 1995 study conducted at the behest of the Virginia General Assembly provides evidence of unfair treatment in the siting of especially large landfills, known as "mega-landfills," and in landfill enforcement activity. Evidence from other areas of the country is more mixed. Studies conducted at the national level and in Massachusetts have not found that municipal solid waste facilities are located disproportionately in low-income or minority communities.

Still, many landfills around the United States that receive MSW from hundreds of miles away are located in sparsely populated, economically vulnerable areas. When we consider the policy problems associated with trash transport, we must ensure that communities hosting landfills or incinerators are treated fairly. The final part of chapter 3 describes normative principles that have been set forth in the environmental justice literature and describes their application to MSW facilities.

The Congress's concerns take center stage in chapter 4, which describes legislative efforts to regulate the interstate transport of trash. I also discuss private and public sector reactions to these proposals. Policy solutions that have been introduced over the past fifteen years fall into two basic categories. Some legislative solutions would allow local governments to capture the flow of trash and to direct it to specific local facilities, a practice known as "flow control," while other legislative proposals would permit state governments to impede trash sent from other states. The most recent bills have dropped the notion of granting the right to flow control and have focused on various forms of state restraints—for example, capping the amount of non-state MSW dumped at state facilities or taxing out-of-state MSW.

In chapter 5 I use the information set forth in previous chapters to arrive at a problem statement and the matching policy solutions. I conclude that MSW transport across state lines is not problematic in and of itself. For example, trash moving between the District of Columbia and neighboring central Virginia does not seem objectionable on environmental or ethical grounds, because the two regions are reasonably close to one another and because the District of Columbia is much more densely populated than are many parts of Virginia. Taxing out-of-state waste more than in-state waste does not make sense, even on the grounds, for example, that New Yorkers have not paid taxes in Virginia and therefore are underpaying for the environmental services that Virginians now and in the future are supplying. Garbage generated in other parts of Virginia and dumped in landfills elsewhere in the Commonwealth has environmental and social effects as detrimental as those generated by out-of-state garbage. Finally, some local governments have come to rely on the income generated by landfills located in their communities, in part because schools and other public services in these areas are not sufficiently supported through property taxes or by state funding.

However, even in the land-rich United States, we should be concerned about trash that moves hundreds of miles, because that movement creates air and water pollution. Long-distance transport also violates even a mild version of the proximity principle, which advocates taking care of waste close to its point of generation. We should also worry about the disproportionate burden that is placed on low-income and minority populations, whose cash-strapped communities often invite landfills as last-resort development opportunities.

In my view, the policy problems to be solved are as follows: we are foisting costly environmental problems onto our children and grandchildren by burying huge amounts of trash that will inevitably cause air, land, and water pollution; we do not sufficiently encourage waste reduction; some MSW travels hundreds of miles to its point of disposal; and low-income and minority communities too often bear the environmental and social burdens of trash disposal. To address these problems I suggest that the national government undertake the following actions: impose a tax on every ton of trash generated in the United States; establish national goals for decreasing MSW production; regulate the disposal of electronic devices and household hazardous waste, since these components of MSW contain especially hazardous compounds; and institute new political protections for potential or actual host communities so that they can make informed decisions and so they will receive fair compensation.

The federally imposed garbage tax envisioned here would be collected at disposal facilities and redistributed to state and local governments. We know that landfills eventually leak (many Superfund sites were once garbage dumps), and thus the tax revenues should be directed to "trash Superfund" accounts that will assist our children and grandchildren in dealing with the future effects of our waste. To address the problem of long-distance transport, state governments should be allowed to escalate the federal trash tax as a function of the distance the trash travels, thereby providing an incentive for trash-exporting local governments to find disposal facilities closer to home and for trash generators to make less garbage. The revenues from such escalator taxes should be shared with local governments hosting MSW disposal facilities, because their revenues could decrease as escalator taxes increase. Trash taxes will also provide an incentive for MSW generators to divert waste and to reduce the amount of waste generated.

To level the playing field for communities that are potential or actual mega-landfill sites, EPA should establish empowerment offices that would provide information on health and environmental issues and on fair compensation. EPA already provides grants for expert assistance in communities with Superfund sites, and a similar program should be established for MSW sites so that community members may obtain independent advice that is framed in laymen's terms. States should be required under the RCRA (Resource Conservation and Recovery Act) solid waste planning process to demonstrate that low-income and minority communities are not disproportionately affected by MSW disposal.

Finally, I suggest that the United States Environmental Protection Agency study the viability of implementing a version of the proximity principle here in the United States. That principle, which dictates that MSW be disposed as close to its point of origin as possible, is a cornerstone of garbage management policies in the European Union and in Japan.

CHAPTER 1

All Garbage Is Local

Trash Management in the United States

Speaker of the House Tip O'Neill was fond of saying that "all politics is local." With this pithy phrase Mr. O'Neill was conveying both an observation and a prescription. First, he was stressing that local and regional concerns are often key factors in national elections. And, second, he was observing that politicians must consider those concerns as they craft national policies.[1]

In a variant of Speaker O'Neill's observation, we might also say that all garbage is local. Trash management is overwhelmingly under state and local control in the United States. As such, any analysis of municipal solid waste management in the United States must start and end with federalism, for American waste management is highly decentralized and as a consequence it varies widely from locality to locality.

For more than a century operational responsibility for municipal solid waste collection and disposal has fallen on cities, townships, and counties.[2] States develop environmental standards for landfills and incinerators that must be at least as stringent as those established by the United States Environmental Protection Agency. But for the most part there is little national oversight. Municipal solid waste management in the United States is overwhelmingly a local and state concern.

Despite this constant of political decentralization, new variables are transforming the American waste management equation.[3] Waste disposal is becoming increasingly privatized and regionalized and, as a result, trash is moving over long distances and across state lines as never before. These trends have not gone unnoticed by members of Congress, many of whose constituents are frustrated that their states have become the trash capitals of the country.

This chapter provides basic information on MSW's composition and environmental impacts, and it describes how MSW is regulated and managed in the United States. I then discuss trends in garbage transport and the connections between those trends, more stringent environmental regulation, and increasing privatization of MSW disposal.

Environmental Effects of MSW

"Solid waste" is a broad term, including discarded hazardous and nonhazardous materials in solid or liquid form. Interestingly, while municipal solid waste has been the focus of much policy and regulatory activity, it represents but a small fraction of the overall solid waste generated in the United States. Informal EPA estimates show that approximately five billion tons of "non-wastewater waste" are generated in the U.S. every year, an amount that includes 214 million tons of industrial non-hazardous wastes.[4] Some industrial waste is discarded on site (e.g., through land application), and some is reused (e.g., scrubber sludge can be used in gypsum production, and fly ash from municipal waste incinerators can be used to fill old mines). The hazardous fraction of industrial waste is sent to special disposal facilities, in accordance with federal regulations.

Because the controversy over interstate waste transport is about municipal solid waste (MSW), I focus on this subset of overall solid waste, and I use "MSW" interchangeably with "garbage" and "trash." With all three terms I refer to the kinds of things we discard in our daily lives, such as product packaging, newspapers and magazines, yard waste, food scraps, clothing, old appliances, batteries, and the like. Residences, commercial enterprises, and industrial operations all make MSW. Some components of the MSW stream—solvents, pesticides, computers, fluo-

TABLE I   Municipal Solid Waste in the United States (2007)

Category of MSW	Percentage of total MSW generated
Paper	32.7
Yard trimmings	12.8
Food scraps	12.5
Plastics	12.1
Metals	8.2
Rubber, leather, textiles	7.6
Wood	5.6
Glass	5.3
Other	3.2

Source: U.S. Environmental Protection Agency, "Municipal Solid Waste in the United States: 2007 Facts and Figures."
Note: Figures represent MSW discarded before recycling or composting.

rescent lightbulbs—would be subject to hazardous waste regulations if discarded on a large scale by industrial generators. However, the household hazardous waste exemption allows Americans to throw into their residential trash bins annually about 1.6 million tons of products containing hazardous materials.

EPA's figures indicate that in 2007 Americans produced about 254 million tons of MSW overall, or 4.6 lbs/person-day. Table 1 shows how this waste breaks down by type. According to EPA, this national breakdown has not varied much since 1960. However, these figures represent national averages, and many local waste profiles look quite different, especially for areas with especially low or high amounts of yard waste.[5]

Even though MSW might seem relatively innocuous by comparison to industrial hazardous waste, when buried or burned MSW can have damaging effects on air quality and water resources. These health and environmental risks can be substantial. In a 1984 report, EPA estimated that "of the municipal solid waste landfills studied, more than 500 violated groundwater standards, 845 violated air quality standards, and 660 were cited for surface water contamination."[6] Most MSW disposal in the United States involves immediate landfilling: in 2007, 81 percent of MSW that was not recycled or composted was landfilled, and the remaining 19 percent was burned, often for energy recovery. Incinerator ash is then reused or disposed of in landfills.[7]

Gases emanate from landfills, either because they evolve from the waste itself or because they are formed as decompositional products. The EPA estimates that 33 percent of all human-generated methane in the United States comes from landfills. The greenhouse gases methane and carbon dioxide are the gases that occur in the highest concentrations in landfills, but they are accompanied by a host of trace compounds that cause landfills' obnoxious odors (sulfides), that contribute to smog formation (volatile organic compounds), and, in the case of benzene and vinyl chloride, are known human carcinogens.[8]

These gases cause other deleterious effects. When landfill gases displace oxygen in the soil, plants can be harmed, because less oxygen is available for uptake by their roots. Methane at landfills has long been a source of concern because it tends to migrate away from the landfill into surrounding areas or buildings, where it can cause explosions at high enough concentrations. On-site methane-induced fires can occur, too.[9] Methane's potential to exacerbate global warming has sparked new interest in controlling its migration from landfills. However, landfill methane is a potential energy source as well, because it can be burned to generate electricity or heat. According to EPA, there are 445 landfill methane-to-energy projects in the United States and an estimated 535 landfills are good candidates for such projects.[10]

Municipal waste incinerators are popular in many European Union Member States and in Japan because they reduce trash volume by 70 to 80 percent and because the heat of combustion can be used to generate electricity or steam. There are 107 MSW incinerators in the United States, approximately 400 in the EU, and 1,490 in Japan.[11] Ash from the combustion of municipal waste takes up less room in landfills relative to original waste, an important consideration in densely populated countries with little land to spare. However, uncontrolled air pollution from municipal waste incinerators contains particulate matter, carbon monoxide, nitrogen oxides (which are smog precursors), dioxins, furans, cadmium, mercury, lead, and acid gases. Modern air pollution controls aim to reduce those emissions substantially.[12]

The solid waste residues associated with MSW combustion typically amount to 25 percent of the weight of the original trash stream. The ash produced by municipal waste incinerators consists of bottom ash, fly ash, boiler and economizer ash, and air pollution residue. Bottom ash

Three municipal solid waste incinerators in Tokyo, Japan: Shibuya Ward (*top*); Toshima Ward (*left*); and Yokohama Ward (*bottom*). (Photos by Itaru Okuda, used by permission)

includes "grate siftings," which are fine materials that pass through the grate at the bottom of the combustion chamber. Fly ash shows concentrated levels of toxic heavy metals like cadmium, lead, and chromium, raising concerns that these contaminants might leach from landfills accepting incinerator ash into groundwater or nearby surface waters. There are ongoing efforts in the scientific community (especially in the EU and in Japan) to understand better the leaching characteristics of ash from municipal waste incinerators.[13]

Landfill leachate is the liquid that collects in landfills primarily as a result of rain infiltration and groundwater intrusion. Chemicals leached from MSW landfills include a wide variety of heavy metals (mercury, lead, chromium, and cadmium), nutrients (nitrogen compounds), and organic substances. Old, unlined MSW landfills are notorious for oozing toxic stews into the surrounding environment, and many of them have been added to the national list of Superfund sites. Hurricane Katrina inundated several Superfund sites in and around New Orleans, including the infamous Agriculture Street Landfill that accepted hazardous and non-hazardous wastes for decades and is now a source of many toxic compounds.[14]

Because of the contamination associated with older, unprotected landfills, EPA has used its statutory authority under the Resource Conservation and Recovery Act (RCRA) and the Clean Air Act to set national standards for landfills and for municipal waste incinerators. RCRA's landfill standards, first established in 1991 after Congress mandated them in the 1984 Hazardous and Solid Waste Amendments to RCRA, impose the following restrictions: (a) landfills may not be located near certain kinds of areas, e.g., geological faults and wetlands; (b) landfills must have a "composite liner," which consists of a 60-mm-thick geoplastic liner over two feet of compacted soil; (c) a leachate collection and removal system must be installed; (d) methane levels must be controlled so that no explosions occur; (e) the waste must be covered frequently with soil, to reduce odors and to control vermin; (f) regular groundwater monitoring must be conducted; (g) the landfill operators must have an approved plan for closing the landfill and maintaining it safely for thirty years after closure; (h) if groundwater is contaminated beyond a certain point, the operator must take "corrective action"; and (i) the operators must demonstrate the financial ability to undertake closure and post-closure care. For landfills whose emissions exceed 50 Mg (metric tons) of volatile organic compounds annually, Clean Air Act standards further require gas collection and destruction systems that will reduce volatile organic compound emissions by 98 percent. States can implement stricter landfill standards, if they so choose. For example, New York State requires a double composite liner for MSW landfills.[15]

Municipal waste incinerators are also regulated under RCRA and the Clean Air Act. RCRA standards apply to incinerator ash, which has been the subject of litigation that reached the United States Supreme Court. In *City of Chicago v. Environmental Defense Fund* (511 U.S. 328 [1994]), the Supreme Court overturned EPA's policy of exempting MSW incinerator ash from hazardous waste tests. That exclusion had been based on the Congressional exemption of household hazardous waste from RCRA's hazardous waste provisions. But the Supreme Court's decision means that MSW incinerator operators must now test the ash from their facilities to make sure it passes toxicity standards. Waste that flunks this test must be sent to hazardous waste facilities. Most of the seven million tons of MSW incinerator ash generated annually passes these tests, allaying industry fears that ash disposal costs would skyrocket, and much ash is treated to neutralize its toxic elements.[16]

Under the Clean Air Act's Section 111, EPA has established standards for large new MSW incinerators and emission "guidelines" for existing MSW incinerators, which the States must use to develop equally strict regulations. Gases regulated under these provisions include particulate matter, cadmium, lead, mercury, acid gases, hydrogen chloride, dioxins/furans, nitrogen oxides, and sulfur dioxide.

THE SPECIAL PROBLEMS OF ELECTRONIC EQUIPMENT

When we imagine MSW in the twenty-first century, electronic waste surely looms as one of the newest, most daunting problems. Despite the many environmental precautions undertaken to protect water, land, and air from potential contamination from municipal solid waste disposal, electronic waste presents a unique threat to human health and the environment.[17]

TV and computer tubes contain the toxic metals lead, cadmium, and mercury, compounds that can be dangerous even in low quantities. For example, cathode ray tubes contain about four pounds of lead each. Furthermore, discarded electronics represent wasted natural resources because they contain precious metals like gold, silver, and platinum that could be reused rather than buried underground. The energy savings of recycling electronic equipment could be substantial. The Government Accountability Office (formerly, General Accounting Office) reports that perhaps 80 percent of the energy consumed in the entire life cycle of a computer (including manufacturing) could be saved through reuse.

Consumers wishing to dispose safely of used electronics must generally pay to do so. Their alternative is to store outdated electronics or to toss them in the trash can, which in most areas of the country remains legal and is even recommended because household waste is exempt from RCRA's hazardous waste provisions. For example, when I called local authorities in my hometown of Charlottesville, Virginia, to inquire about recycling a used computer, I was told to simply put it into the garbage can. Eventually, I found a local electronics store that would take my used electronics for a fee ranging, from ten to twenty-five dollars per item. This particular commercial enterprise promises that they use a domestic recycling operation rather than sending the items overseas, where too often they are dismantled by the poor under unsafe and environmentally hazardous conditions. But sending electronics to developing nations is not always a bad thing. Many functional cell phones discarded by affluent Westerners looking for an upgrade are reused in the developing world.

The immensity of the disposal problem associated with used electronic equipment is staggering, as illustrated by the following statistics:

- Americans own three billion pieces of electronic equipment.
- Electronic waste comprises 2 percent of the municipal solid waste stream, and that percentage is likely to rise.
- One reliable forecast predicted that a hundred million computers and monitors would become obsolete in 2003, a threefold increase over 1997 levels.
- Twenty million televisions in the United States become outdated every year, a number that will undoubtedly rise as digital TVs come into more widespread use.
- The United States Geological Survey has estimated that in 2005

there were half a billion unwanted cell phones languishing in desk drawers in the United States and that their worth in terms of precious metals was about $300 million.

• EPA estimates that 1.5 to 1.9 million tons of e-waste were discarded in 2005.

While the evidence suggests that most people are simply storing their old electronics for now, at some point those devices will emerge from storage.

The fate of such devices is of great concern, given that under-recycling electronic equipment is costly and that equipment sent overseas is likely to be disassembled under unsafe conditions. Workers in developing countries are often exposed to toxic contaminants, despite the fact that U.S. export regulations specify that receiving countries must be notified about such contaminants and must consent to receiving the used equipment. The GAO has recommended that EPA take the following actions to help promote domestic recycling and reuse of electronic equipment: (1) develop a nationwide financing system to reduce financial barriers to recycling and reuse; (2) ensure that cathode ray tubes are subject to existing export restrictions; and (3) take more steps to broaden federal government involvement in e-waste recycling and reuse.

As of 2008 EPA had not implemented those recommendations and a national stakeholder group had reached an impasse over how to finance recycling and reuse schemes. However, several states have stepped into this regulatory breach. As of 2007, fourteen states had adopted e-waste legislation or regulatory programs, and many more have proposed legislation. These actions vary widely, but they include bans on landfilling or incineration, consumer or producer fees to finance recycling or reuse, and setting environmental standards for recycling operations.

Federalism and MSW Disposal in the United States

Although many political programs in the United States have been nationalized in the past century, the United States remains a federal system that clings to the notion of decentralized responsibility and states' rights. This dedication to federal principles is vividly illustrated in the complicated legal framework that dictates how Americans manage their trash. While the national government sets minimum environmental standards for landfills, federal laws delegate most responsibility for trash management to state and local governments.

The 1976 Resource Conservation and Recovery Act, or RCRA, provides the applicable federal legal framework. Subtitle D of RCRA sets forth the provisions that apply to trash management, and by contrast with the tight, nationally controlled systems for hazardous waste and underground storage tank management specified under other subtitles, Subtitle D places responsibility for MSW management on states and local governments, as follows: "The objectives of this subtitle are to assist in developing and encouraging methods for the disposal of solid waste which are environmentally sound and which maximize the utilization of valuable resources including energy and materials which are recoverable from solid waste and to encourage resources conservation. Such objectives are to be accomplished through Federal technical and financial assistance to States or regional authorities for comprehensive planning pursuant to Federal guidelines designed to foster cooperation among Federal, State, and local governments and private industry."[18] EPA's role for MSW management under RCRA has been to establish a national floor for landfill environmental standards and to provide technical guidance for the states as they develop federally required plans, regulations, and permits for their municipal solid waste and non-hazardous industrial waste facilities.

Budget expenditures are good indicators of administrative priorities, and the relatively low funding amounts devoted to MSW management reinforce the federal government's statutory dependence on state and local authorities for trash management. EPA's publicly available budget data are not fine-grained enough to determine exactly how much the Agency devotes to Subtitle D programs. In 2008, however, EPA requested about $82 million for "waste management" and "waste management/recycling," categories that likely encompass activities devoted to MSW, and other kinds of waste too. Even so, this figure is revealing, for these two categories constitute barely one percent of EPA's total budget request of $7.2 billion.[19]

While state governments set standards and develop statewide plans for managing MSW disposal facilities, municipal governments are ultimately responsible for managing MSW generated within their bound-

Open roadside dump near Panama City, Panama, 2008. (Photo by author)

aries, and they have been assuming this public responsibility since the late 1800s. Local officials charged with managing trash have employed a long list of disposal solutions that were sometimes inventive but not always environmentally or economically wise.

Filling land, especially coastal areas, was a favorite use of garbage for many years, and many American cities have extended their boundaries into nearby waterways by mixing garbage with other materials. While this has created new and often desirable space in coastal cities, these filled-in areas can be physically unstable, especially in earthquakes. Incineration was first popularized about a century ago, as was a technique known as reduction, which promised to transform garbage into usable materials, but which ultimately proved expensive and smelly and thus fell into disuse. Other disposal methods that were widely used at some point during the twentieth century were ocean dumping, pig farms, and, of course, the "sanitary" landfill, so called because the trash is covered with soil. Although MSW management has come a long way in the United States, illegal roadside dumping still occurs.[20]

The decentralized nature of MSW management translates into many different approaches to waste disposal and recycling, and each approach is adapted to local circumstances. For example, many local governments export waste to nearby localities or to other states, presumably as a function of high local costs and/or political resistance. The State of California has banned the disposal of electronic and hazardous wastes. Some cities have established aggressive recycling programs, while others have not mounted similarly ambitious efforts.[21]

The decentralization of MSW management and recycling also means that there is no standardized method for estimating recycling rates, which can be calculated to include only the residential fraction, or both residential and commercial fractions. So "apples-to-apples" comparisons are not always possible with recycling. Still, a recent survey by a waste trade magazine showed that recycling rates in U.S. cities range widely, from below 25 percent in Dallas, Detroit, Columbus, Houston, Indianapolis, Phoenix, and San Antonio, to above 60 percent in Los Angeles, San Francisco, and San Jose. While local circumstances and recycling costs vary considerably, a relatively recent EPA analysis found that the social benefits of achieving a 35 percent recycling goal nationwide likely outweigh the costs by a greater than three to one margin.[22]

Many municipalities have boosted their recycling rates through pay-as-you-throw programs, which charge for waste disposal on a per-unit basis. These programs create incentives to discard less trash, recycle more, and consume less stuff. The benefits can be substantial. Portland, Oregon, increased its recycling rate from 7 percent to 35 percent within one year of implementing a pay-as-you-throw program. The town of Dover, New Hampshire, reported saving more than $300,000 annually in waste disposal costs. And Mt. Vernon, Iowa, saw a 40 percent decrease in waste collected between 1990 and 1995.[23]

TRASH ON THE MOVE: THE RISE OF THE MEGA-LANDFILL

While local innovation and flexibility are laudable effects of the decentralized nature of MSW management in the United States, some observers are increasingly uncomfortable with a system that makes some states the trash repositories for other states. How this has happened demonstrates another reality of the American federal system: the move-

TABLE 2   State Imports of Municipal Solid Waste (2005 or latest year)

State	MSW Imported (tons)
Pennsylvania	7,931,984
Virginia	5,709,441
Michigan	5,442,044
Indiana	2,428,838
Wisconsin	2,143,133
Illinois	2,114,898
Oregon	1,795,971
Georgia	1,744,317
New Jersey	1,731,729
Ohio	1,689,470
South Carolina	1,243,993
Total (top 11 states)	33,975,818
Total (all 50 states)	42,194,795

Source: U.S. Congressional Research Service, *Interstate Shipment of Municipal Solid Waste: 2007 Update.*

ment of commerce among the states is protected under the Constitution, and the Supreme Court has affirmed recently its oft-stated assertion that trash is commerce.

Trash is on the move as never before in the United States, and there is no sign that the trend is abating. Further, a few states have absorbed the bulk of exported trash. As shown in table 2, eleven states import individually greater than 1,000,000 tons annually; and collectively these top eleven states account for 81 percent of trash imports.[24] The congressional delegations from these states have led the charge for legislation that would allow state or local governments to constrain the movement of trash across their borders.

Trash is on the move partly because many disposal facilities have closed in the past two decades. According to *Waste Age* magazine, these closures occurred largely because their owners could not meet at reasonable cost the modern environmental standards required by national and state regulations. At least 5,000 closures occurred between 1988 and 1997, and 40 percent of these were concentrated in Texas, Virginia, Wisconsin, and Alaska. There are now approximately 1,800 operating landfills and about 107 MSW incinerators in the United States.[25]

Although some observers feared a waste disposal crisis when thousands of landfills closed, newer landfills tend to be sized to handle tremendous capacity and to be located farther from the point at which the garbage is generated. Many of the closed landfills were publicly owned and operated, and they were small and poorly protected from leaks and gas releases. New landfills in the United States are more likely to be privately owned and/or operated, they must meet much more restrictive environmental standards, and they are likely to be enormous. The sheer size of these so-called mega-landfills has attracted attention to the phenomenon of long-distance transport. One recently built Virginia landfill could in theory grow to be five hundred feet tall, which is the height of the Washington Monument, and it could extend across an area equal to a thousand football fields. Virginia now hosts fifteen mega-landfills, ten of which are concentrated in the southeast quadrant of the state.[26]

Mega-landfills are one manifestation of consolidation and privatization in the waste management industry. The GAO estimates that as recently as 1992, only 13 percent of non-metropolitan landfills and 24 percent of metropolitan landfills were privately owned and operated. Historically, most municipalities owned and managed their own facilities as public enterprises. Waste hauling was frequently contracted out to private firms, but they tended to be local and relatively small. This profile has changed dramatically in the past fifteen years. Many municipalities have moved to privatization in an attempt to cut costs, improve efficiency, and sidestep the financial burdens of meeting Subtitle D regulations at their own facilities. By 1998, 36 percent of MSW landfills were privately owned and 58 percent of MSW was disposed of in private landfills.[27]

The waste industry is dominated by three national firms: Waste Management, Allied Waste Industries, and Republic Services. These large national businesses increasingly offer a wide array of services, including waste collection, recycling, and disposal, and to keep costs down such companies prefer to use their own landfills or incinerators, no matter how far from the trash's point of origin, even if this means gathering trash from a multistate region.[28]

Mega-landfill operators can take advantage of the economies of scale, which make high-volume, low-area landfills the most profitable. As one observer has put it, "Landfill costs directly relate to area and landfill profits derive from disposal volume." In concrete terms, one 2005 analysis estimated that a landfill receiving 10,000 tons per year would cost

$83/ton to operate, while one landfill receiving 300,000 tons per year would cost $14/ton. Mega-landfills help to keep disposal prices relatively low, even in the face of construction costs that range typically from $300,000 to $800,000 per acre, depending on site characteristics. One recently developed method for holding disposal costs down involves the high-tech equivalent of stepping on a wastebasket's contents: by piling and then removing mounds of dirt onto garbage, landfill operators can literally squeeze garbage into smaller spaces than before.[29]

While waste management firms defend the economies of scale possible with huge waste disposal facilities, a concern in Virginia (and elsewhere) is that the communities hosting these huge private landfills are disproportionately rural, poor, and minority. Many of the Virginia communities with mega-landfills are desperate for revenue to support their schools and other public services. In those cases, state funding and revenues from local property taxes are insufficient to support strong schools and public services. Such communities are therefore vulnerable when landfill companies approach them with offers of landfill host fees, and the companies are well aware of this fact.[30]

Closure of one notorious aging landfill has helped focus politicians' attention on the interstate transport of trash. In 1996 New York City Mayor Rudy Giuliani abruptly decided that the Fresh Kills Landfill, which was the largest operating landfill in the world, should be shut down. In its operating life, Fresh Kills had covered more than two thousand acres on Staten Island, and it was allegedly the largest man-made feature on earth, visible from space and eclipsing even the Great Pyramids and the Grand Coulee Dam. By one estimate, over a twenty-year period the unlined Fresh Kills Landfill had discharged several billion gallons of leachate (landfill "juice") into New York Harbor. For all intents and purposes, Fresh Kills was closed for good in early 2001, though it reopened later that year to provide a site for sifting through and disposing of the World Trade Center debris.[31]

New York City now transports almost three million tons of trash annually outside the City's limits, which has provoked well-publicized political resistance in states that receive the City's trash. In New Jersey, Governor Christie Todd Whitman, who later became President George W. Bush's first EPA Administrator, bristled at the suggestion that New Jersey should accept New York's garbage. Virginia's Governor James

Gilmore responded with lawsuits when Mayor Giuliani suggested that Virginians should welcome New Yorkers' trash in exchange for the Big Apple's cultural offerings. In the midst of this acid exchange between Gilmore and Giuliani, one Virginian observed wryly that "When people say Yankee trash, they think it's redundant."

A series of *Washington Post* and *New York Times* articles followed the back-and-forth sallies between Governor Gilmore and Mayor Giuliani, highlighting some of the associated issues, such as increased truck traffic on interstate highways, the presence of illegal medical and industrial wastes, and leaking barges. Since the late 1990s national press coverage has been minimal, with the exception of a 2007 *Marketplace* series of public radio stories on consumer culture. But local newspapers in areas with huge landfills, and books like Elizabeth Royte's *Garbage Land,* continue to turn an occasional spotlight on the issue.[32]

THE DORMANT COMMERCE CLAUSE QUESTION

A central issue complicating the regulation of long-distance transport of MSW in the United States is a series of U.S. Supreme Court decisions holding that garbage transport is a commercial activity that merits constitutional protection. Under the "dormant Commerce Clause" of the Constitution, states may not erect barriers to interstate commerce unless the Congress has explicitly allowed it. The dormant Commerce Clause is not explicit in the Constitution, but rather is the logical, if unstated, implication of that document's admonition under the Commerce Clause, that "the Congress shall have Power . . . to regulate Commerce . . . among the several States."[33]

In several cases dating back to the late 1970s, the Supreme Court repeatedly overturned state or local solid waste laws on grounds that they impermissibly interfered with interstate commerce. Some laws were found to "facially discriminate" against interstate commerce, while others were found to fail the "Pike test," which allows some incidental interference with interstate commerce if there is a genuine local public interest at stake. In the 1978 *City of Philadelphia* decision, in which New Jersey was forced to lift its ban on out-of-state garbage, the Court described its views on the Pike test: "If a legitimate local interest is found then the question becomes one of degree. And the extent of the burden that will be tolerated will of course depend on the nature of the local interest involved, and on whether it could be promoted as well with a lesser impact on interstate activities."[34]

Since deciding *City of Philadelphia,* the Court until quite recently consistently affirmed lower-court decisions that struck down state or local interference with waste transport. An Alabama tax on out-of-state hazardous waste, a Michigan policy that attempted to conserve landfill capacity, and an Oregon fee on out-of-state garbage were all overturned by the Court. Chief Justice Rehnquist dissented in each case, arguing that the states were in each case trying to protect a legitimate health or environmental interest. In the Michigan case, Justices Rehnquist and Blackmun asserted in their minority opinion that states with relatively low population density have no obligation to accept trash from more crowded states.[35]

Notable in this series of cases is *C. A. Carbone v. Town of Clarkstown.* In this decision the Supreme Court invalidated a flow control ordinance enacted by Clarkstown, New York, under which all garbage collected in the town had to be taken to the town's waste transfer station, which was leased to a private company. At waste transfer stations, garbage collection trucks unload trash so that it can be stored temporarily until loaded onto larger vehicles for further transport. Sometimes recyclable materials are sifted from the waste stream at such facilities. Many cities enacted similar flow control ordinances, whose purpose was to ensure a large enough revenue stream to support public bonds or to subsidize recycling and waste-reduction efforts, which often do not pay for themselves. In the wake of the *Carbone* decision, some local governments found themselves unable to pay off the public debts incurred in building sophisticated waste handling facilities because they could no longer keep trash at home.[36]

In the post-*Carbone* world, market forces have strongly channeled where waste is taken for disposal, and state and local regulatory restrictions focusing on transport have faced judicial limits. A 2001 decision addressing Virginia laws followed this pattern. In 1999 Governor James Gilmore and the Virginia legislature enacted five new provisions that would have capped the amount of waste allowed in Virginia landfills, prohibited barge transport of trash, and regulated truck transport of trash. Waste Management, Inc. sued the Commonwealth, and a federal

The Oneida-Herkimer Convenience Center in Utica, New York. The sign lists the wide range of MSW recycling, composting, and waste disposal services offered by the Oneida-Herkimer Solid Waste Management Authority. (Photo by author)

appeals court largely affirmed a lower-court decision overturning the restrictions. Because the restrictions affected only waste transported from outside the state, they were held to violate the dormant Commerce Clause.[37]

However, a recent Supreme Court decision reflects a shift in the Supreme Court's views on flow control. In April 2007 the Court upheld ordinances enacted in the New York counties of Oneida and Herkimer that directed the flow of all locally generated trash to a local public transfer station. The counties' solid waste management authority argued that there was no violation of the dormant Commerce Clause, because the local ordinances discriminated equally against competing in-state and out-of-state facilities that might otherwise receive the local waste, and because the transfer station was operated by a public entity. They asserted further that their ordinances served important local interests—for example, promoting a comprehensive recycling program and handling local waste in an environmentally safe manner.

In a split decision, the Supreme Court agreed with the counties and their waste management authority. The Court upheld the flow control ordinances, relying heavily on the fact that the transfer station was operated by the local governments, not a private entity. "States and municipalities are not private businesses—far from it," Chief Justice Roberts wrote for the majority. "Unlike private enterprise, government is vested with the responsibility of protecting the health, safety and welfare of its citizens. . . . Given these differences, it does not make sense to regard laws favoring local government and laws favoring private industry with equal skepticism."[38]

Determining the Public Interest

The United States Congress has regularly considered legislation permitting state or local governments to control the movement of trash. The policy concerns underlying these efforts are: the dramatic increase in long-distance transport and its negative consequences; the fact that some cities are sending vast amounts of trash to faraway disposal facilities concentrated in a handful of states, like Virginia and Pennsylvania; the mind-boggling size of some regional mega-landfills; and judicial constraints on the ways in which state and local governments may control trash movement. Some legislative proposals would have reinstated flow control authority to localities that had adopted it prior to the 1994 *Carbone* decision, whereas others would allow state governments to restrict the flow of waste imported from other states.[39]

These concerns have consistently crossed party lines. For example, in 1999, Virginia's U.S. senators (one Republican, one Democrat) jointly sponsored legislation that gave local communities the right to reject imported garbage; allowed state governors to cap garbage imports at 1998 levels or to block imports from "super-exporting" states like New York; and provided for taxes on imported garbage. More recently introduced bills vary in their provisions, but they reflect similar goals. HR 274, introduced in early 2007 by the late Representative Jo Ann Davis (R-VA), would enact a presumptive ban on interstate imports unless specifically authorized by a host community agreement, and would allow states to restrict the amount of out-of-state waste received annually at each waste facility.

Canadian imports have become a political target, too, to the point that during the 2004 presidential campaign, Senator John Kerry pledged, if elected president, to ban the importation of Canadian trash into Michigan. Companion bills passed in the House and introduced in the Senate would allow any state to restrict garbage imports from another nation until the Administrator of the Environmental Protection Agency issues regulations implementing and enforcing the Agreement Concerning the Transboundary Movement of Hazardous Waste between the United States and Canada. To date, Michigan is the only state affected by this bill, and the intended target is Canadian trash exports to Michigan.[40]

Thus far, the federal executive branch has stayed out of the interstate trash legislative debate. Both the Clinton and the Bush administrations declined to take a position on the issue. The solid waste management industry is adamantly opposed to any restrictions on its trade.

Congressional discussions all revolve around one central question: should we restrict the interstate trade of trash? To a student of the American political system, this way of framing the problem might seem to contradict contemporary environmental policymaking practice. Thirty years ago we wondered if we should leave air and water pollution control in the hands of state and local agencies, but now that question seems antiquated. We now accept that we should control pollution that can move between states, and we have incorporated this recognition into programs like the Clean Air Act's provisions for acid rain, which aim to reduce the airborne transport of sulfur dioxide and its atmospheric products, and the Clean Water Act's restrictions on industrial polluters, which are based in part on the principle that industrial discharges in one state should not interfere with another state's ability to achieve water quality standards.[41]

While American politicians are generally willing to regulate pollution that moves across political boundaries, they are clearly conflicted over whether to regard trash primarily as pollution or as commerce, and their proposals reflect that uncertainty. Legislative solutions differ depending on whether the public interest is equated with facilitating a freely operating market, with allowing local governments autonomy over landfill siting and trash management, or with protecting state landfill capacity and natural resources.

There is yet one more way of framing the policy problem to be solved. In political fights over where garbage should go, national, state, and local decision makers should consider more seriously the possibility that trash transport across state borders might not be the central problem. Trash is on the move not only because of landfill closures, regionalization, and privatization, but also because Americans produce a lot of garbage. Perhaps therein lies part of the policy problem.

CHAPTER 2

Waste Not, Want Not

Are Americans the World's Premier Waste Makers?

"Trash" is a relative concept.[1] The meaning of the term varies depending on the time and on the circumstances. Historian Susan Strasser demonstrates that through the late nineteenth century Americans evinced a strong attachment to the ideas of thrift and reuse. All classes embraced these notions, which were exemplified in New York City's commitment to source reduction.[2]

But in the early twentieth century, Americans became more inclined to discard goods rather than mend or recycle them. In effect, we came to perceive used items and food waste as unwanted, and, in so doing, we redefined our ideas about what constituted trash. This inclination was reinforced when advertisers in the 1920s began to present throwaway products as convenient and sanitary. As Strasser puts it, "The ideal of the durable and reusable was displaced by aspirations of leisure and luxury, ease, and cleanliness."[3]

Strasser's work points to the close links between waste disposal and consumption. Her work complements that of Vance Packard, who more than forty years ago condemned practices like planned obsolescence, constant changes in fashion, and advertising that encouraged consumption for its own sake. Packard was concerned that artificially induced consumption would turn us all into "waste makers." Whether or not we agree with Packard's obvious distress over what he called a "force-fed society with a vested interest in prodigality," we should heed his admonition to consider patterns of consumption and their connection with waste production.[4]

In this chapter I consider first the theoretical and empirical relationship between consumption and pollution. In so doing, I focus on the debate among environmental economists over whether increased economic activity, as measured by consumption levels and GDP, is associated with predictable changes in environmental degradation. Then I examine empirically the question of whether Americans make more trash than their European Union and Japanese counterparts. Finally, I describe the ways in which the EU, its Member States, and Japan constrain trash management through integrated, multifaceted regulatory strategies.

Does Prosperity Make Us Better Environmentalists?

Logic suggests that the more we consume, the more pollution we make. The laws of thermodynamics tell us that higher energy expenditure is associated with more waste. One way to advertise one's affluence to friends and neighbors is to discard lots of objects. In fact, there is little dispute that at low levels of economic development, consumption, economic growth, and pollution are positively related. However, there is controversy over whether economic growth eventually helps environmental quality or whether affluence is the environment's worst enemy. There are many voices on both sides of this argument.[5]

E. F. Schumacher's rallying cry in *Small Is Beautiful* is that economic growth, long the central goal of economists because it is seen as the antidote to poverty, is inevitably detrimental to the environment. Arguing along parallel lines, the economist Herman Daly asserts that economic growth as traditionally construed cannot be sustained because natural resources are finite. Similarly, Ehrlich and Ehrlich claim that unchecked population growth and unfettered consumption in the developed nations will cause environmental disaster. To these influential observers, economic growth in developing and developed countries alike inevitably poisons the environment because rich people consume more per capita than do people of lesser means. Phrased another way, these observers believe that with affluence inevitably comes an "effluent" society.[6]

However, many economists believe that as we become more prosperous, pollution per capita or per unit of GDP increases at first, but then decreases at higher income levels. When graphed, this relationship between per capita GDP and per capita pollution looks like an "inverted U," or a bell. Adherents of the inverted-U hypothesis assert that at low to intermediate levels of affluence, pollution rises with consumption, but that at higher levels of affluence, pollution decreases per unit of economic productivity.[7]

The theory underlying this somewhat counterintuitive prediction works as follows: as their incomes rise, people are more willing to pay for products that are made in environmentally protective ways, and are also more likely to demand government intervention to reduce pollution levels and to protect natural resources. In addition, pollution-abatement techniques are likely to become less expensive in more-affluent economies because of investments in research and development and thus, the richer we are, the more likely it is that these more-cost-effective technologies will be used. According to the most fervent subscribers to the inverted-U hypothesis, economic growth is the salvation of the environment and poverty is the environment's main enemy. In other words, all we need do is grow out of our polluting ways.[8]

Other adherents of the inverted-U hypothesis make more nuanced claims. Grossman observes that economic growth's effect on pollution and natural resource use depends on several factors. According to Grossman, pollution that creates immediately observable, localized effects is likely to become publicly salient and, therefore, capture political attention. Such pollutants will probably be regulated, and thus their emissions and ambient concentrations will decrease with affluence. By contrast, pollutants that travel to distant places or whose impacts are less immediately palpable to the general citizenry (e.g., gases that lead to climate change) are less likely to be effectively addressed by politicians. As Grossman puts it, "Output growth may impart continuing harm to the environment along those dimensions where the adverse consequences will be shared widely by peoples in different regions or countries, or where the effects on health and welfare will not be evident until well into the future."[9]

Anecdotal examples from developing and developed countries alike verify the expectation that the impoverished tend not to be concerned with environmental protection, and that rising affluence at lower income levels leads to greater pollution. China is growing economically by leaps and bounds, but the average Chinese remains relatively poor. Air pollution in China today causes an estimated 400,000 premature deaths each year, and that number could rise to 550,000 by 2020.[10] During the era of Soviet domination in Eastern Europe, forests died over large areas in Czechoslovakia, Poland, and East Germany as a result of acid rain that was linked with the uncontrolled burning of coal. Developing countries suffer from rampant deforestation by people who have no other way to survive than by selling lumber or growing crops on cleared plots.[11]

Before strong air pollution regulation was instituted in more-affluent countries, severe air pollution episodes in Donora, Pennsylvania (1948), the Meuse River Valley in Belgium (1930), and London (1956) killed or sickened hundreds of people. In steel-manufacturing areas like Gary, Indiana, families could not hang out their laundry on high-pollution days, because it would become dirty again almost immediately. Every beginning biology textbook tells the tale of the peppered moth, whose predominant coloration patterns have changed from light to dark and back to light over the past 150 years in part because of the initial presence—and now absence—of heavy soot pollution, which formerly darkened tree trunks and made it easy for predators to extinguish light-colored moths.[12]

These and other, similar examples seem to confirm the inverted-U-shaped relationship between affluence and pollution. But there is a lively debate in the literature about whether this relationship even exists, and if it does, about the underlying causes. Air quality is generally much improved today in the United States and in the European Union relative to what it was a few decades ago, a trend that would seem to support the inverted-U hypothesis. The best evidence for the inverted-U relationship is for two kinds of air pollution, sulfur dioxide and particulate matter, and for lead and fecal coliform concentrations in rivers. However, for many other pollutants—carbon dioxide, carbon monoxide, nitrogen oxides, mercury in water, arsenic in water—concentrations or emissions continue to increase with per capita income. Other research casts doubt on whether the inverted-U exists for any pollutant. Because of data limitations these analyses are generally performed across nations of varying GDPs at one point in time, as opposed to within nations across time.[13]

Even for pollutants like sulfur dioxide, whose localized levels have declined in many countries, it sometimes happens that the problem is shifted geographically without reducing overall emissions. In the United States and elsewhere electric power plants have installed stacks hundreds of feet tall to improve nearby concentrations of sulfur dioxide and particulate matter, but this widely employed dispersion technique has created the long-distance problem of acid rain. In response to the environmental damage caused by the migration and chemical transformation of pollution across long distances, Congress mandated sharp cuts in utility plant sulfur dioxide emissions in the 1990 Clean Air Act Amendments. By 2006 sulfur dioxide emissions from power plants were 40 percent lower than those in 1990. Those congressionally mandated reductions were followed by the even more stringent Clean Air Interstate Rule sulfur dioxide and nitrogen oxides regulations enacted by EPA and the states.[14] After an initial period during which sulfur dioxide emissions were effectively shifted from one area to another in the United States, recent regulatory efforts have successfully reduced overall emission and deposition levels.

We will likely continue to see situations in which environmental problems are shifted within or between countries without reducing overall pollutant load. Consumers in rich countries sometimes find ways of sending their pollution abroad, thus making it appear that environmental quality has improved when, overall, it has deteriorated. For example, while domestic resource extraction per capita in the EU-15 Member States grew very little between 1992 and 2002, indicating a decoupling from growth in GDP, some heavily polluting industry simply moved from Europe to developing nations like China. Such results, if widely realized, would undermine the contention that overall pollution is reduced as income increases, and it would point to a future in which developing nations will find it difficult to find still-poorer countries to use as dumping grounds.

A final caveat to the inverted-U hypothesis is that even if per capita pollution decreases in accordance with the theory's predictions, population growth can cause aggregate pollution to rise. And it is aggregate pollution, not per capita pollution, that causes environmental harm.[15]

Where we observe environmental improvements with increasing income per capita there is still the question of underlying cause. Is economic growth per se responsible for lowered pollution, or are other factors like regulatory programs or population control responsible? Selden et al. analyzed declines in air pollution emissions in the United States between 1970 and 1990 in an attempt to determine the underlying causes. Their conclusion was that the policies and programs flowing from the Clean Air Act caused the greatest pollution reductions, while purely economic ("compositional") effects played a much smaller role. Some analyses indicate that social equality measures (civil rights, income equality, or educational levels) are linked more strongly with lower pollution levels than is economic growth. Some argue that there is nothing automatic about the relationship between economic growth and pollution. Rather, population growth is the main force causing increased pollution. In this view, controlling pollution levels means controlling birth rates, which tend to drop as countries become wealthier and as education levels rise, and promoting policies that reduce pollution produced per person or per unit of GDP.[16]

A final point of contention concerns the role of technological change in pollution control and natural resource conservation. Some techno-skeptics argue that technological advances are likely to worsen pollution and natural resource degradation because pollutants like synthetic organic chemicals and smog are more damaging than the pollution created by earlier technologies. In this Malthusian view, economic growth and technological change in recent decades have created more, not less, environmental damage, and thus we cannot depend on "progress" to save us from environmental devastation. The World Bank is among the prominent institutions arguing the opposite view—that technological change coupled with sensible regulatory policies can foster economic development that is compatible with environmental improvement.[17]

When one looks closely at the research, it becomes clear that neither economic theory nor measured relationships point to an unequivocal relationship between economic growth and pollution levels. Growth can degrade the environment and lead to higher rates of natural resource consumption, but it is also true that pollution is most likely to become publicly salient among the relatively affluent, who do not have to worry as much about basic needs. Citizens in the more-prosperous industrialized countries have successfully pressured politicians to deal with pollution that is visible and easy to link with local or regional detrimental effects.

Examples of environmental incidents that galvanized public attention include: the oily pollution that caused the Cuyahoga River to burst into flames, which happened periodically in the 1950s and 1960s when floating petroleum levels became high enough to cause surface ignition; the many acutely toxic smog and particulate matter episodes that occurred in the U.S. in the middle part of the twentieth century; the catastrophic 1984 Bhopal gas leak; the 1986 meltdown of the Chernobyl nuclear power plant; and the 1989 *Exxon Valdez* spill. However, citizens and politicians in affluent nations may pay less attention to pollution that is simply shoved out of most people's sight and dumped on a few. Trash would seem to fall into this latter category and, thus, this is one type of pollution that might increase with economic growth at all levels of development.

In this next section I examine closely the empirical relationship between per capita generation of municipal solid waste and per capita GDP. In this work I rely on research undertaken with Dr. Itaru Okuda, who has provided unique access to, and analysis of, Japanese documents on MSW generation.

THE RELATIONSHIP BETWEEN AFFLUENCE AND TRASH GENERATION

While the inverted-U hypothesis may hold for some types of air and water pollution, it is not at all clear that the rich nations produce less trash than poor nations.[18] In a cross-country comparison, Shafik found that municipal waste produced per person increases with per capita income at all levels. In 1995 average municipal waste generation per capita in the less-affluent EU-12 was 79 percent of that in the relatively wealthy EU-15. By 2005 this gap had widened, not narrowed, so that average MSW generation in the EU-12 was only 58 percent of that in the EU-15, largely because overall per capita trash generation in the prosperous EU-15 has continued to rise while that in the less-wealthy EU-12 fell slightly between 1995 and 2005. A recent survey of the literature on the connection between income and MSW generation concluded that there is scant evidence of an inverted-U-curve with MSW. In Italy, a turning point (downward inflection) in the relationship between income and MSW is apparently reached only at €22,000–€31,000 value added per capita, levels that are seen in only the wealthiest Italian provinces.[19]

The analyses presented in this section examine the ways in which waste-generation and management patterns vary with income levels and across nations. An important, related question is whether Americans truly deserve their reputation for excessive wastefulness relative to their equally affluent counterparts in the industrialized nations. Even a century ago it seemed that Americans were more wasteful than Europeans. Environmental historian Martin Melosi has found that early twentieth-century urban Americans produced almost twice as much rubbish per person relative to the English and more than double the per capita amount observed in many German cities.[20]

Widely cited data indicate that this relationship continues into the present day. Environmental data published by the Organisation for Economic Cooperation and Development (OECD) have consistently shown that Europeans and the Japanese produce much less trash than do Americans. For example, OECD's most recent environmental compendium indicates that, on a per capita basis, Americans make more trash than do the citizens of any other OECD country and that each American makes 750 kg of trash annually, or 32 percent more than the average EU-15 citizen (570 kg/year) and 88 percent more than the average Japanese (400 kg/year).[21] From these comparisons it would seem that Americans have earned a justifiable reputation as careless waste makers and despoilers of the earth and that Americans' famously high level of consumption is matched by a correspondingly high rate of MSW generation.

But these oft-cited statistics invite a closer look. Cross-national comparisons of environmental data are often complicated by dissimilar measurement techniques, or simply by different definitions of what constitutes waste. Such discrepancies are noted scrupulously by the sponsoring agencies, but it is generally impossible to do more than hand-wave in the general direction of such ambiguities because many international organizations generally report without alteration the data contributed by their member countries. In the following analysis, I present the first close comparison of MSW generation and recycling patterns in the United

States, Japan, and the European Union, and I correct for different ways of defining MSW. This analysis represents the first attempt to translate Japanese estimates so they are comparable with European and American data on municipal solid waste.[22]

BACKGROUND DATA AND ASSOCIATED UNCERTAINTIES

As has been the case throughout this book, "municipal solid waste" (MSW) here includes the kinds of materials that land in residential and commercial trash. The MSW data reported here do not include waste from industrial processes, construction, demolition, or renovation debris, nor do they include agricultural waste or sewage sludge.[23] The terms "garbage," "trash," and "MSW" are used synonymously.

The two most often cited sources for MSW generation in the U.S. give quite different figures. On the one hand, the Environmental Protection Agency reports that Americans produced 251 million tons (or 227,000,000 Mg) of MSW in 2006, for an average of 0.84 tons (0.76 Mg) per person annually. On the other hand, Simmons et al. estimate that Americans produced 388 million tons of MSW generated in 2004, for a much higher annual per capita generation rate of 1.35 tons (1.22 Mg).[24] Not surprisingly, these varying figures rely on entirely different methodologies, and deciding which data to use demands an understanding of how they were generated.

EPA's data come from Franklin Associates, who estimate MSW generated through a materials flow methodology that, in top-down fashion, combines information about the amounts and estimated life of all materials consumed annually. Franklin Associates has applied the same method since the 1960s, so these data have the virtue of consistency over many years and they explicitly exclude construction-related debris. They do not include water discarded with products.

In contrast, Simmons et al. use a bottom-up, direct methodology that relies on each individual state's records on waste disposal. While these figures would appear to be a more accurate reflection of waste disposed, many states do not have the administrative resources to accurately track MSW generation. Furthermore, states rely on differing techniques to estimate waste disposed and they may include different kinds of waste under the heading "MSW." A reporter for a leading waste trade journal commented on Simmons's estimates as follows: "The problem with state data is that the 50 states define and count garbage differently. . . . For instance, according to their [Simmons's] data, each resident of Indiana created 2.1 tons of trash in 2004, while each Ohioan only created 1.4 tons. Are Hoosiers the garbage kings of America? The most likely answer is that Indiana counts trash differently than Ohio."[25]

While the EPA figures appear more reliable than the Simmons et al. data, EPA's figures underestimate the size of the MSW stream, because they exclude materials like water that are added to, and disposed with, consumer products. According to one set of estimates, water can comprise 5 percent of the weight of garbage.[26] At the same time, EPA's data include MSW disposed from any source, including industrial operations.

Comparing MSW data from the U.S. with that in the EU is complicated by the fact that the Member States report and collect data differently from one another. European authorities indicate that reporting across countries has not always been consistent in terms of the kinds of waste streams included as MSW. Efforts are under way to harmonize data collection so that statistics from the various EU Member States are comparable.[27]

The data presented for Japan have been adjusted to make them comparable to those for the United States and the European Union. The legal definition of MSW in Japan is narrower than comparable definitions in the United States and Europe, and the Japanese Ministry of Environment's data also exclude a large part of recyclables collected through private routes. Because the Japanese government reports data quite precisely and descriptively, it has been possible to increase the official estimates of waste generated and recycled so as to include privately collected MSW, thereby ensuring a more accurate estimate of MSW generated.

WASTE-GENERATION AND MANAGEMENT PATTERNS I:
INTERNATIONAL VARIATION

Municipal waste generation and recycling figures for the United States, the EU-15, and Japan are displayed in tables 3 and 4.[28] Several interesting cross-national contrasts are immediately apparent. Table 3 indicates that each American makes at least 29 percent more—and perhaps as much

TABLE 3   Annual Per Capita Rate of MSW Production in the U.S. (2002 and 2004), EU-15 (2002), and Japan (2002)

	U.S.		EU-15	Japan
	EPA data (2002)	Simmons data (2004)	(2002)	(2002)
MSW (tons/Mg)	0.83/0.75	1.35/1.22	0.63/0.58	0.62/0.57

Sources: European Commission, *Europe in Figures: Eurostat Yearbook, 2006–7*; Okuda, "State of Waste Management in Japan"; U.S. Environmental Protection Agency, "Municipal Solid Waste in the United States: Facts and Figures for 2006"; Simmons et al., "State of Garbage in America." See text for an explanation of the differences between the EPA and the Simmons data.
Note: More recent data are unavailable for Japan.

as 110 percent more—MSW than his or her Western European or Japanese counterpart. Table 4 shows that in 2002 average recycling rates were reasonably similar in the EU-15 and the U.S., but that Japan's recycling rates were substantially higher. Japanese government authorities have made increasingly aggressive attempts to foster even higher recycling rates.[29] But the EU-15 Member States have pulled ahead of the U.S. in the past several years. As of 2005 the EU-15 Member States had as a whole substantially increased the amount of waste diverted to recycling and composting, exceeding by 10 percent comparable levels in the U.S. in 2006.

A drawback of broadly average recycling figures is that they mask regional variations. A look at a finer scale reveals that some states and nations have pursued recycling and composting more aggressively than others:

- In 2006, Seattle, Washington, had achieved a 53 percent recycling and composting rate.[30]
- In 2008, Florida governor Charlie Crist signed a bill setting a 75 percent recycling goal for the year 2020.
- The City of San Francisco aims to send zero waste to landfills by 2020. The City has already managed to divert 69 percent of its MSW from landfills, through a combination of reuse, prevention, recycling, and composting.[31]
- By 2005, Belgium had achieved a 58 percent recycling and composting rate, and in 2006, 70 percent of waste in the Flanders region of that country was diverted to recycling or composting.[32]

Table 4   Recycling Rates (percentage of MSW generated) in the U.S., EU-15, and Japan

Year	U.S.	EU-15	Japan 2002
2002	29	29	35
2005/2006	33[a]	43[b]	n/a
	(2006)	(2005)	

Sources: U.S. Environmental Protection Agency, "Municipal Solid Waste in the United States: Facts and Figures for 2006"; European Environment Agency, "Municipal Waste Generated Per Capita, 1995–2005"; Thomson and Okuda, "Garbage In, Garbage Out: Virginia Is for Landfills."
[a]Includes composting.
[b]Includes composting. Figures were computed by subtracting from total MSW generated the amount of MSW sent to landfills and incinerators.

- In 2005, recycling plus composting rates in Denmark, Germany, and the Netherlands were 41 percent, 65 percent, and 66 percent, respectively.
- Denmark, Finland, Germany, Greece, and Switzerland all achieve greater than 50 percent recycling rates for one or more of their waste packaging streams.
- In the United States as a whole in 2007, 55 percent of paper and paperboard products were recycled and 64 percent of yard trimmings were composted.[33]

As these figures show, recycling has become embraced strongly in the developed world, despite occasional periods when recycling markets have been oversaturated and despite lingering questions about whether the overall social benefits of recycling outweigh the costs. In response to such questions, in 2002 the U.S. EPA, several commercial organizations, and state agencies co-sponsored a study of recycling's economic impacts. The study concluded that the recycling industry is directly or indirectly responsible for four million jobs. Further, the report concluded that recycling's environmental benefits can be identified at every stage of product use, ranging from the lower energy consumption that results from lower virgin resource extraction, to lower greenhouse gas emissions from landfills because of reduced waste disposal, to less need to incinerate or dump MSW in the ground, and to stimulating the development of green technologies. In *Why Do We Recycle?* Frank Ackerman adds that even when recycling does not pay for itself, it is still good to invest in a variety of recycling technologies that could be key components of future environmental strategies, if and when virgin natural resources become more limited or more expensive to extract.[34]

Much of the economics literature discussed at the beginning of this chapter posits that as affluence rises, the public's interest in environmental issues also increases, causing politicians to respond with programs that reduce pollution or natural resource use. Based on this speculation, and considering that MSW generation tends to rise with affluence, we might expect recycling rates to increase along with the amount of waste produced.

However, figure 1 shows that this relationship is actually quite variable across nations, pointing to the importance of nationally specific conditions in waste management decision making.[35] For example, because plastics packaging is replacing metal packaging, overall recycling rates are likely lower in some countries, like the U.S., where metal cans are recycled at rates of 49 percent for aluminum and 64 percent for steel, but where plastic bottles are recycled at the much lower rate of 33 percent.[36] It is illuminating to examine some of these cross-national differences more closely. In the following comparisons, U.S. and EU data are for 2004 and Japan data are for 2002:

- Belgium and Sweden produce low amounts of MSW annually (465 kg/capita and 464 kg/capita, respectively) while achieving high recycling rates (58 percent and 44 percent of MSW generated, respectively).
- Denmark, Germany, and Austria also recycle high percentages of their MSW (41 percent, 58 percent, and 58 percent, respectively), but the citizens of these countries produce relatively high amounts of waste (696 kg/capita, 600 kg/capita, and 627 kg/capita annually).
- The U.S. and the UK produce relatively high amounts of MSW per capita (750 kg/capita and 600 kg/capita annually), but their recycling rates are relatively modest (29 percent and 23 percent, respectively).

The data shown in tables 3 and 4 point to a strong contrast in waste generation and recycling patterns between the United States and Japan.

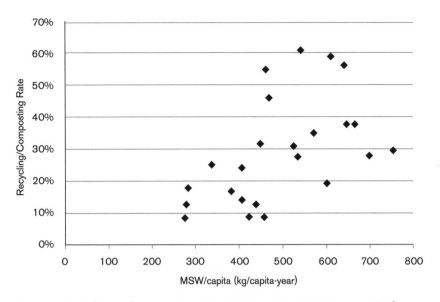

FIGURE I. Recycling and composting rate vs. MSW generation rate (2002) in the U.S., EU, and Japan.

Source: European Commission, *Europe in Figures: Eurostat Yearbook 2006–7*. EU Member States for which data were available are Austria, Belgium, Czech Republic, Denmark, Germany, Estonia, Finland, Greece, Spain, France, Ireland, Italy, Latvia, Hungary, the Netherlands, Poland, Portugal, Romania, Slovenia, Slovakia, Sweden, and the United Kingdom.

Anecdotal observations reinforce these differences. Food portions in Japan are smaller than those routinely served in the United States, likely leading to less organic waste in Japan. Eating out is much more common in the United States than in Japan and Japanese children are discouraged from leaving food on their plates, at home and at school. It is difficult to throw things away in Japan, while in most of the United States it is easy to discard almost anything at any time. Used electronic equipment in Japan is taken back to the store for recycling, a practice that is only slowly being adopted across the United States. Finally, plastic cups, utensils, and plates are rarely used in Japan, but their use is widespread in the United States.[37]

The high recycling rates reported for Japan make sense in light of concerted joint efforts by Japanese government authorities and industries. For example, glass bottle and steel can manufacturers report that their manufacturing processes use 83 percent recycled content. In 2001 Japan passed one of the first "take-back" laws for major appliances. Most

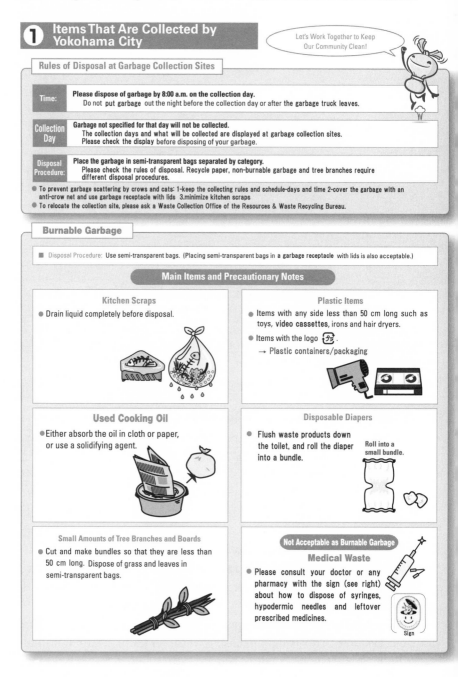

1 Items That Are Collected by Yokohama City

Let's Work Together to Keep Our Community Clean!

Rules of Disposal at Garbage Collection Sites

Time:	**Please dispose of garbage by 8:00 a.m. on the collection day.** Do not put garbage out the night before the collection day or after the garbage truck leaves.
Collection Day	**Garbage not specified for that day will not be collected.** The collection days and what will be collected are displayed at garbage collection sites. Please check the display before disposing of your garbage.
Disposal Procedure:	**Place the garbage in semi-transparent bags separated by category.** Please check the rules of disposal. Recycle paper, non-burnable garbage and tree branches require different disposal procedures.

● To prevent garbage scattering by crows and cats: 1-keep the collecting rules and schedule-days and time 2-cover the garbage with an anti-crow net and use garbage receptacle with lids 3.minimize kitchen scraps
● To relocate the collection site, please ask a Waste Collection Office of the Resources & Waste Recycling Bureau.

Burnable Garbage

■ Disposal Procedure: Use semi-transparent bags. (Placing semi-transparent bags in a garbage receptacle with lids is also acceptable.)

Main Items and Precautionary Notes

Kitchen Scraps
● Drain liquid completely before disposal.

Plastic Items
● Items with any side less than 50 cm long such as toys, video cassettes, irons and hair dryers.
● Items with the logo [プラ].
 → Plastic containers/packaging

Used Cooking Oil
●Either absorb the oil in cloth or paper, or use a solidifying agent.

Disposable Diapers
● Flush waste products down the toilet, and roll the diaper into a bundle.
Roll into a small bundle.

Small Amounts of Tree Branches and Boards
● Cut and make bundles so that they are less than 50 cm long. Dispose of grass and leaves in semi-transparent bags.

Not Acceptable as Burnable Garbage
Medical Waste
● Please consult your doctor or any pharmacy with the sign (see right) about how to dispose of syringes, hypodermic needles and leftover prescribed medicines.
Sign

FIGURE 2. How to put out your garbage and recyclables in Yokohama City, Japan.
Source: http://www.city.yokohama.jp/ne/life/en/garbage.html.

Dry-Cell Batteries

▣ Disposal Procedures: Use semi-transparent bags. (Separate dry-cell batteries from other garbage.)

▣ Main Items: Manganese batteries, alkaline batteries and lithium primary batteries.

▣ Precautionary Notes: Button-type batteries and rechargeable batteries are not collected.

Spray Cans

▣ Disposal Procedures: Use semi-transparent bags. (Separate spray cans from other garbage.)

▣ Main Items: Hair spray, insecticide, gas cassettes, etc.

▣ Precautionary Notes: ● Do not pierce the can.
● Before disposal, empty the can completly in a safe place with lots of ventilation / air flow and away from heat.

Non-burnable Garbage

▣ Disposal Procedures: Place items in the box or wrap them in a thick paper, and label the contents that you have wrapped. For example : 'ガラス (glass)' or '蛍光灯(fluorescent light)'.

▣ Main Items: Glass, ceramics, fluorescent lights, light bulbs, etc.

Plastic Containers/Packaging

▣ Disposal Procedures: Use semi-transparent bags.

▣ Main Items: All items with the "plastic containers/packaging " logo 🄬 .

▣ Precautionary Notes: ● Rinse the insides to remove any residue. Remove any metal/paper label.
● For food trays, bring them back to collection boxes at cooperating supermarkets.

What Does "Containers/Wrapping" Mean?

Containers and packaging (wrapping) that are no longer needed after taking out the products within.

Bottles	Squeezable containers	Nets	Trays
Bowls/Dishes	Caps	Plastic Bags/ Food Wrap	Plastic Cushioning Materials

Inapplicable Items

● Products themselves (such as video cassettes , toys, wash basins).
  → Burnable Garbage

● Extremely soiled items.
  → Burnable Garbage

● Plastic PET bottles.
  → Cans, Bottles and Plastic PET Bottles

of the financial burden in this system is shared by manufacturers and the government, rather than consumers. Furthermore, Japan has instituted aggressive household separation and recycling programs. In Yokohama, a city of 3,500,000 people, trash must be sorted into ten different categories and grieving pet owners must pay a fee to have their pet's remains taken away. Yokohama's detailed instructions for separating trash are shown in figure 2. Korimatsu, a town of 2,200, requires that residents sort their trash into forty-four separate categories. Japan's ultimate goal is to achieve a closed-loop economy in which waste products in one area become inputs to another.[38]

Disaggregated data on specific waste streams are not reported regularly for any of the countries under examination here. However, those available for paper and glass in the mid-1990s reinforce the conclusion that, at least at that time, Americans were more wasteful than Western Europeans, although the differences narrow if only high-income European countries are included in the comparison. The European Environment Agency (EEA) estimates that when averaged into three like groups, its fourteen member countries consumed on average from 130 kg to 210 kg of paper per capita in 1995, with the highest single country level at 260 kg per capita. By contrast, average U.S. consumption and disposal for paper was 285 kg per capita in 1995. In 1995 each American tossed away on average 40 kg of glass containers, while between 1990 and 1995 Europeans in the fourteen EEA countries discarded a low of 10 kg per capita to a high of 40 kg of glass containers per capita.[39]

One might reasonably ask if Americans make more trash simply because they are more economically productive. In other words, are we seeing borne out the observation that trash per capita rises inexorably with GDP? The answer to this question appears to be that among the world's wealthiest nations, MSW generation per capita rises as a function of GDP per capita. Figure 3 and table 5 both depict MSW/capita as a function of GDP/capita for the U.S., the EU-15, and Japan. A straight line plotted through the points displayed in figure 3 would show the change in MSW per unit of GDP. As shown in table 5, if we use EPA's data for MSW generation in the United States, one-half of the countries included in this analysis produced as much or more waste per unit of GDP and the other half produced less waste per unit of GDP relative to the United States. Rates of MSW production per unit of GDP are rela-

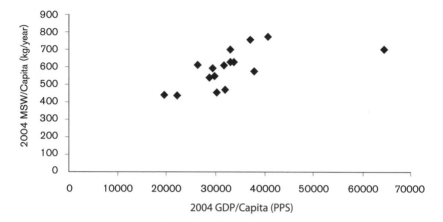

FIGURE 3. GDP/capita vs. MSW/capita for the U.S. (2004), EU-15 (2004), and Japan (2002). (MSW data for Luxembourg, represented by the point with the highest GDP/capita, were estimated, not reported, for 2004. PPS stands for "purchasing power standards," a measure that allows direct purchasing-power comparisons by correcting for price differences.)

Sources: European Commission, *Europe in Figures: Eurostat Yearbook 2006–7*; Okuda and Thomson, "Regionalization of MSW Management in Japan"; U.S. Environmental Protection Agency, Office of Solid Waste, "MSW in the U.S.: 2007 Facts and Figures."

tively low in Japan compared with those in many EU Member States and in the United States.

Luxembourg stands out both in figure 3 and table 5 for that country's seemingly low production of MSW per unit of GDP. However, these figures are misleading. Luxembourg's per capita production of MSW in 2005 was 705 kg/capita, which puts that country far above the EU-15 average of 567 kg/capita. Luxembourg's GDP counts the productivity and earnings of more than 120,000 foreign commuters who make up more than half of the working population.[40] Much of the MSW produced by those workers is generated and disposed at their homes in adjacent EU Member States. This means that MSW produced per capita in Luxembourg is undercounted relative to GDP generated per capita.

The U.S. data used in figure 3 are from the EPA. Using these data, the United States does not show the highest levels of MSW production per unit of purchasing power. If we use instead the Simmons et al. data, generation of MSW in kilograms per $1,000 of PPS soars to 30.5, which would be the highest generation rate of all the industrialized nations, exceeding by two times that in Belgium and Finland.

TABLE 5   Rankings for MSW/GDP for the U.S. (2004), EU-15 (2004),
and Japan (2002)

Country	MSW/GDP (kg/1,000 PPS[a])
Luxembourg	10.8
Belgium	14.6
Sweden	14.7
Finland	15.1
Japan	15.1
France	18.4
Netherlands	18.6
Italy	18.8
United States (EPA data)	19.1
Austria	19.1
United Kingdom	19.1
Greece	19.6
Germany	20.5
Ireland	20.4
Denmark	21.2
Portugal	22.3
Spain	23.2
United States (Simmons et al. data)	30.5

Sources: European Commission, Europe in Figures: Eurostat Yearbook 2006-7; Okuda and Thomson, "Regionalization of MSW Management in Japan"; U.S. Environmental Protection Agency, Office of Solid Waste, "MSW in the U.S.: 2007 Facts and Figures."
Note: For the United States, both EPA data and Simmons et al. data are for 2004; data for Japan are for 2002.
[a]PPS stands for "purchasing power standards," a measure that allows direct purchasing-power comparisons by correcting for price differences.

WASTE-GENERATION AND MANAGEMENT PATTERNS II:
HISTORICAL AND PROJECTED TRENDS

Another way of evaluating the relative magnitude of MSW generation in the United States is to examine historical trends. An important confounding factor when considering historical trends in MSW data is that they are expressed terms of weight, not volume. Containers and packaging make up 31 percent of MSW and thus shifts in packaging weight can have an important impact on apparent MSW generation rates. In the past few decades we have switched from heavier packaging such as steel and other metals to lighter packaging materials made of plastics. Between 1960 and 2006 steel packaging in the MSW stream decreased by

TABLE 6   MSW Generation Trends in the United States

Year	MSW Generated (thousand Mg/year)	MSW/Capita (kg/person)	MSW/GDP (kg/$1,000)
1960	79,907	445	31.9
1970	109,838	540	29.1
1980	137,501	607	26.6
1990	186,116	748	26.2
2000	216,410	769	22.0
2006	227,929	761	20.1

Sources: U.S. Department of Commerce, Census Bureau, "USA Quick Facts"; U.S. Department of Commerce, Census Bureau, "Your Gateway to Census 2000"; U.S. Department of Commerce, Bureau of Economic Analysis, "National Income and Product Accounts Tables"; U.S. Environmental Protection Agency, "Materials Generated in the Municipal Waste Stream, 1960 to 2006."

41 percent, from 4,660 tons in 1960 to 2,750 tons in 2006, while plastics packaging increased by more than one hundred times, from 120 tons in 1960 to 14,230 tons in 2006. Average weights within types of packaging have also decreased. Between 1972 and 1992 soft drink beverage containers decreased in weight by 18 percent (plastic), 22 percent (aluminum), 31 percent (steel), and 36 percent (glass). This trend continues as manufacturers seek to develop packaging of all kinds that is lighter and therefore cheaper to produce and to transport. For example, between 1995 and 2000 approximately one hundred billion aluminum cans were shipped annually in the United States, but the weight of that reasonably constant number of cans dropped by 6 percent over the same period.[41] Given recent fluctuations in fuel prices, this trend seems likely to continue. However, the lightening of packaging implies that we are discarding more individual items than implied by weight-based MSW statistics.

Table 6 uses EPA estimates, since they extend back to 1960, and those data show that Americans produced 73 percent more MSW by weight per capita in 2006 than they did in 1960. However, MSW generated per capita has increased only slightly since 1990 and it actually dropped a bit between 2000 and 2006. Further, because GDP rose much faster than did population, the amount of trash produced per $1,000 of GDP dropped by 37 percent between 1960 and 2006.[42]

As is the case in the U.S., trash production per person seems to be leveling out in the European Union. This change could be attributable to ongoing aggressive efforts in many EU-15 Member States to reduce the production of MSW. Other factors unrelated to waste reduction might also be at work. For example, to the extent that MSW statistics include waste disposed by industrial operations, movement of manufacturing operations to the developing world would cause domestic MSW statistics to decrease even if the overall amount of MSW produced from those operations stays the same and is merely dumped elsewhere. Many types of industrial operations have moved from the EU to the developing world, although countries like Germany have counteracted this trend with subsidies that have attracted auto manufacturing and semiconductor operations. Packaging is becoming lighter in the EU, as is the case in the United States. It is also possible that techniques used to estimate MSW may have formerly underestimated the relative fraction of light (e.g., plastics packaging) MSW and overestimated the heavy (e.g., ash) fraction. Efforts to correct MSW estimates on the basis of improved statistics may give the erroneous impression that less waste is being produced.[43]

Projections based on recent patterns indicate that between now and 2020 MSW generation in the EU will continue to grow more, but more slowly than GDP. EU officials expect that by 2020 MSW generation will increase by 22 percent in the EU-15 and by 50 percent in the new EU-10 Member States, respectively, while GDP is expected to grow by 35 percent in the EU-15 and by 75 percent in the EU-10.[44]

Considered together, the international and historical analyses presented above point to the following conclusions:

- Each American generates at least 29 percent more MSW than his or her Japanese or average European counterpart.
- Trash generated per person and per unit of GDP tends to rise with affluence and consumption, although some nations have enacted waste management policies that have counteracted these tendencies.
- Each American makes substantially more trash than he or she did in 1960. But in the past several years MSW production per capita has leveled out in the United States and in the EU-15.
- In the United States and the EU-15 trash production is growing more slowly than GDP.

- These slower MSW generation rates could stem from a number of causes, including: the movement of manufacturing operations to the developing world; aggressive recycling, waste reduction, and reuse policies; changes in MSW estimation techniques; the "light-weighting" trend in packaging; or a combination of these factors.
- Americans recycle much more vigorously than ever, albeit at a level lower than that achieved in Japan and when compared to the EU-15 Member States as a whole. Recycling rates and programs vary considerably around the United States, depending on state and local laws.

The trend toward lighter packaging started many years ago and it seems likely to continue as manufacturers seek lower-cost production and transportation solutions. But this trend complicates the way we view historical trends in MSW generation. For most products there is no reliable way of knowing how the weight of MSW generated correlates with the amount of stuff discarded. The most recent aluminum industry figures available show that we are not introducing fewer cans into the waste or recycling streams, even as the overall weight of aluminum can waste decreases.

WHY EUROPEANS AND THE JAPANESE MAKE LESS TRASH THAN AMERICANS

It is reasonable to speculate that some of the cross-national differences just noted might be connected with waste disposal costs, which vary widely among the industrialized nations. Current average MSW disposal costs in Japan are about \$374/Mg, in part because there are so many incinerators and landfills. Disposal fees vary quite a bit across the United States, but in the most current (2004) national survey available, the national averages for landfilling and incineration were \$37/Mg and \$68/Mg, respectively. In contrast, EU Member States faced landfill or incineration fees approaching or exceeding \$100/Mg even in the late 1990s. Tipping fees (called "tariffs" in the EU) in Northern Italy reach €100/Mg. Landfill taxes are €75/Mg in the Flanders region of Belgium and €85/Mg in the Netherlands. Denmark imposes a landfill tax of €50/Mg and bans landfill disposal of any waste suitable for incineration.

Incinerator fees in Germany amount to €150/ton of MSW.[45] As these figures demonstrate, MSW disposal is still much cheaper in the U.S. than in other affluent countries.

It would be a mistake, however, to infer that disposal costs account for the differences between American practices, on the one hand, and those in Japan and some EU Member States, on the other hand. Rather, we must look at political, social, cultural, and economic factors to understand why Americans make more trash than many of their counterparts in Europe and Japan and why disposal costs are so much lower in the United States relative to Europe and in Japan.

Consumption is one important economic factor that drives MSW generation. Waste production is also affected by the presence or absence of regulatory pressures to produce less waste. In the sections that follow, I elaborate on these two causal factors. First I show that Americans consume more than citizens in the affluent EU-15 and Japan. Then I describe the ways in which policymakers in Japan and in the European Union have embraced the waste management principles of proximity, self-sufficiency, pollution prevention, producer responsibility, and precaution. Those regulatory choices reflect social and cultural norms that have driven the EU Member States and Japan to pursue related goals: to reduce to a minimum the amount of trash sent to landfills; to produce less garbage overall; and to avoid sending trash for disposal to someone else's back yard.

Factor I: Americans as Consumer "Addicts"

Many prominent observers from a variety of disciplines and ideological points of view have concluded that Americans are avid consumers. Political scientist Benjamin Barber concludes that Americans have succumbed to a culture of forced consumerism that has eroded our sense of our role as citizens. Psychiatrist Peter Whybrow claims that Americans are victims of an out-of-control acquisitiveness that has adverse consequences for our health (e.g., by causing obesity) and is destroying our sense of community. Nationally syndicated columnist David Brooks points to a "period of mass luxury," or "hyper-consumerism," as one of the factors underlying the recent mortgage debt crisis in the United States. Brooks asserts that "America once had a culture of thrift" but that "over the past decades, that unspoken code has been silently eroded."

High levels of consumption don't even bring us satisfaction, according to prize-winning author Jared Diamond, who observes that while per capita oil consumption in the U.S. is double that in the EU, by many measures standards of living are as high or even higher in the EU.[46]

In similar fashion, the sociologist Juliet Schor has proclaimed Americans "overspent." By this she means that we spend lavishly relative to our means and that we consume more than Americans of earlier eras. For example, the typical floor plan for a new home today calls for 2,300 square feet, a 55 percent increase over 1970, even though our families have grown smaller over the same period. Schor calls this phenomenon of spending more than we would like or need to, "competitive consumerism," which she describes as a ratcheting up of the middle-class yearning to "keep up with the Joneses." She draws her conclusions from indirect measures of overspending, that is, from surveys in which Americans have confessed that their personal sense of well-being depends on escalating their lifestyles to the next higher level of affluence.[47]

Schor's claims are buttressed by the more direct measures of savings and consumption presented here, which confirm that Americans save less and consume more than our counterparts in other industrialized nations. Household saving rates in the United States have dropped over the past decade and they remain low in comparison with other industrialized nations—for example, the EU Member States that have adopted the euro as their currency. Figure 4 illustrates the large, consistent difference between the U.S. and Euro-area saving rates. For the most part, saving rates in Japan have closely followed those in the Euro-area. These cross-national differences hold even when inconsistent methods of reporting are accounted for.[48]

Low saving rates in the United States have raised concerns with economists because of the resulting potential for insufficient investment capital. But for the purposes of considering the connection between consumption and the environment, these data emphasize the fact that Americans over-spend and under-save relative to their global counterparts in other wealthy countries. In 2005 the U.S. household saving rate was negative because expenditures exceeded income.[49]

Estimates of food consumption and household expenditures reinforce the portrait of Americans as the world's leading consumers. Citizens in the prosperous EU-15 Member States consumed about 10 per-

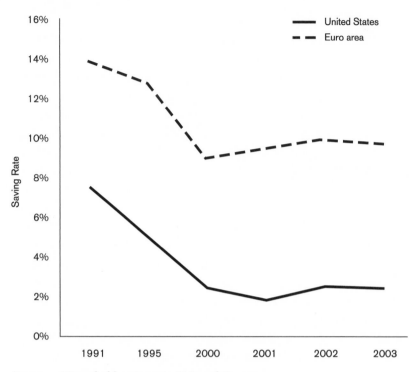

FIGURE 4. Household saving rate, U.S. and Euro-area.

Source: Harvey, "Comparison of Household Saving Ratios."

cent more calories on average in 2001–3 than they did in 1979–81, as contrasted with Americans, whose calorie consumption increased by 19 to 23 percent in the same period, or double the increase seen in the EU. According to the Food and Agriculture Organization's figures, Americans had available to them more calories per capita in 2001–3 than the citizens of any other country in the world. As one point of comparison, 2,770 calories per day were available in food to a Japanese citizen in 2001–3, and 3,770 calories per day were available to an American in the same period. As of 2002, the most recent year for which data were available, Americans spent about 42 percent more in their private lives ($40,677 per "consumer unit," or $16,270 per capita) than did citizens in the EU-15 Member States (€12,000 per capita, or approximately $11,442).[50]

Of course, these data represent the average situation, thereby ignoring the large disparity in the United States between the richest, who can afford to indulge their every desire, and the poorest, who have problems meeting basic needs.

Still, these data point to one conclusion: on average, Americans are in fact relatively voracious consumers. This is part of the reason why we make more trash than our counterparts in the EU Member States and Japan. But regulatory decisions in the EU Member States and Japan also help explain why citizens in those countries make less trash than Americans.

Factor II: How Waste Management Policies in the EU and in Japan Discourage Trash Generation and Movement

For many years the Japanese have subscribed to the proximity principle, which means taking care of waste as close as possible to its point of origin. The proximity principle is nowhere codified formally, but it has become an accepted norm since the "Tokyo Garbage War" erupted in 1971. During that incident one ward in the city of Tokyo refused to accept garbage generated in another ward. Controversies over waste management facilities became so problematic that the governor declared an emergency. Eventually the Tokyo Metropolitan Government decided that the fair solution was to construct incinerators in every ward in the city: since no one wanted garbage, everyone would get it.

It remains standard practice for municipalities in Japan to recover, recycle, incinerate, and dispose of their garbage within their borders, regardless of high costs and inefficiencies of scale. The net result is a reverse image of the "Not-in-my-back-yard" syndrome that results in Japan's having many more landfills and incinerators than are found in the United States.

Japan's population is 40 percent that of the U.S. and its MSW stream is one-third that of the United States, but it has fifteen times as many incinerators and more landfills. Only a small fraction of MSW—435,000 Mg of 72,000,000 Mg tons generated annually, or 0.6 percent—travels across prefecture borders in Japan. In contrast, an estimated 25 percent of MSW disposed of in landfills or incinerators crosses state borders in the United States.[51] The contrast between these two countries is even starker than this comparison indicates, because Japan is the size of California. This difference in geographic scale means that even in the rare instances when trash crosses prefectural boundaries in Japan, it does not move the hundreds of miles that are common with interstate trash transport in the United States.

In essence, the Japanese believe that waste-generators should take responsibility for their own garbage. This dedication to the proximity principle seems to stem from a combination of social and political influences, including: a relatively flat social structure, which discourages social inequity; redistributive fiscal policies, which make rural communities less dependent on trash for cash; strong centralized government control over MSW management, which discourages regional inequities; and inadequate information dissemination and policy evaluation, which has made it hard to compare the effects of different policies. A firm attachment to the proximity principle persists in Japan, even though it is likely much less cost-effective than alternative policies and even though the Japanese central government has promoted regional incinerators because their dioxin emissions are lower than those for smaller, localized incinerators.[52]

In the European Union, the five principles of proximity, self-sufficiency (disposal by Member States of their own waste), producer responsibility, pollution prevention, and precaution (potential risks should be avoided, even if they are not firmly proven) are well established in international and national law and policy. All of these principles are codified in various EU waste directives and regulations, specifically, the Packaging Directive, the Landfill Directive, the Waste Electronic and Electrical Equipment Directive, the Restrictions on Hazardous Substances Directive, the End-of-Life Vehicle Directive, and the Regulation on Transboundary Shipment of Wastes.[53]

Under the Packaging Directive, Member States should have recovered 50 percent of packaging waste by 2001 and the corresponding goal for 2008 is 60 percent. "Recovery" includes recycling or incineration, as long as energy production is involved, although recycling must comprise 55 percent of packaging recovered in 2008. As of early 2008 many Member States had already achieved the 2008 target. Under the Landfill Directive, Member States must reduce biodegradable waste sent to landfills, reaching 35 percent of 1995 levels by 2020, and they must implement certain environmental standards at landfills. The Waste Electronic and Electrical Equipment Directive (WEEE) requires Member States to establish take-back systems for electronic waste such that by the end of 2006 at least 4 kg of waste per person annually are collected separately. WEEE household waste must be collected "at least" free of charge. The complementary Restrictions on Hazardous Substances Directive (RoHS) prohibits as of July 1, 2006 the use of lead, mercury, cadmium, hexavalent chromium, polybrominated biphenyls (PBB), and polybrominated diphenyl ethers (PBDR) in the manufacture of electronic equipment. Finally, the End-of-Life Vehicle Directive restricts the use of certain hazardous substances in vehicle manufacture and requires increased reuse and recovery rates of 95 percent by 2015. If fully implemented, the Landfill, WEEE, Packaging, and End-of-Life Vehicle Directives together will divert more than 40 million Mg of waste from landfills by 2015.[54]

Some EU Member States have pressed ahead aggressively to reduce waste sent to landfills and to limit overall waste generation. In Denmark and the Netherlands, as well as in Switzerland (which is not a member of the European Union), dedicated pollution prevention efforts have decoupled overall waste production from economic growth. By instituting a combination of waste-prevention measures that included public education, taxes, composting, and waste segregation, the city of Dilbeek, Belgium (38,000 inhabitants), decreased disposed (as opposed to recovered) waste by 60 percent between 1995 and 1996. The City estimated that this program saved the municipal government €2 million annually on waste disposal. In the United Kingdom some local governments collect trash only every two weeks, and they limit the amount of garbage that may be set out for collection. Germany is famous for its "Green Dot" (Duales System Deutschland, or DSD) packaging take-back system. The DSD was launched in 1990 and since its introduction it has collected more than 79 million Mg of packaging waste and has recovered 68 million Mg of that waste, at an average per capita cost in 2006 of 29 (euro) cents. Under the DSD 62 percent of Germany's plastics packaging was recycled or recovered for industrial feedstock in 2006, an impressive figure when compared with the plastics packaging recycling figure in the U.S., which was 31 percent in 2006.[55]

The proximity and self-sufficiency principles require EU Member States to strive for self-sufficiency in MSW disposal and to dispose of MSW as close to the point of origin as possible. Regulation of the transboundary shipment of waste codifies these principles into law, subjecting waste shipments for disposal to rigorous requirements that include prior written notification and consent in the importing country. These regulatory hurdles are believed to have halted practically all transboundary movement of MSW intended for disposal. However, MSW destined for recycling or energy-recovery incineration facilities can be exported and imported freely, as these uses are considered beneficial.[56]

The Belgian region of Flanders, with a population exceeding six million, serves as a flagship example for how the proximity, pollution-prevention, and self-sufficiency principles have been woven together. The result is an aggressive, comprehensive management scheme that has achieved low waste generation rates and that has contained waste disposal within the region's boundaries.[57] In conjunction with regional municipalities, the Public Waste Agency of Flanders, or OVAM (Openbare Vlaamse Afvalstoffenmaatschappij), has undertaken the following measures to reduce household-waste-generation rates and to divert as much MSW as possible to recycling or energy-recovery facilities:

- A pay-as-you-throw system with fees ranging up to €1.50 ($2.08 at current exchange rates) per sixty-liter (approximately 15-gal) garbage bag.
- Obligatory separation requirements, with non-compliant bags not picked up.
- Recycling centers ("amenity sites") with twenty to forty bins for different kinds of materials.
- Government provision of home-composting units.
- Widespread distribution of educational materials.
- Producer-responsibility schemes for packaging waste, electronic equipment waste, tires, batteries, vehicles, and other products. (Several of these schemes were initiated through EU directives.)
- Charges of €75/Mg assessed when MSW is sent to landfills, as contrasted with €7/Mg if the waste is incinerated.

These efforts have achieved great success. The Flanders household-waste program boasts a 70 percent recycling and composting rate and a 95 percent rate for overall recovery (recycling, composting, and energy recovery combined). Only a miniscule fraction—5 percent—of household waste generated in Flanders is landfilled immediately.

In Belgium overall MSW generation per capita has grown more slowly than GDP per capita. As table 5 illustrates, Belgium has one of the lowest MSW generation rates per unit of GDP in the EU. Overall MSW generation has leveled out at 531 kg/capita, which is remarkable in light of the fact that in 2007 Belgium had the sixth-highest GDP per capita in the E.U. OVAM aims to reduce "residual waste" (household waste that cannot be recycled, reused, or composted) to 150 kg/capita (330 lbs/cap-

Amenity Site in Belgium. (Photo courtesy of OVAM, Mechelen, Belgium)

ita) by 2010. That goal is within reach, since the residual-household-waste level in 2006 was 153 kg/capita.

Data from various Flanders municipalities indicate that higher pay-as-you-throw fees appear to discourage residual-waste generation. Only 1 percent of residual waste is disposed of illegally. With nine incinerators, Flanders is self-sufficient in waste disposal capacity. Only inert (non-organic) waste can be disposed of in landfills, which reduces methane-generation rates by an estimated 25 Mg annually. The tenfold difference in taxation for disposing of waste in landfills vs. incinerators provides a strong disincentive for landfill disposal.

Despite these successes, Flanders officials do not underestimate the difficulty of long-term efforts to reduce the rate at which households and businesses generate MSW. Patterns of consumption do not necessarily respond even to steep waste fees and that people may tire of separating recoverable materials from trash intended for disposal.

Conclusions

Sometimes one hears the expression, "The data speak for themselves." While this observation might be true in some situations, it could not be farther from the truth when it comes to unraveling the question of whether Americans make too much trash. The response depends on which data are analyzed, on how closely those data are scrutinized, and on how one defines "too much."

If "too much trash" is taken to mean, "more than our counterparts in equally affluent nations like Denmark, Germany, the UK, and Japan," then the answer to the above-stated question is yes. Each American makes at least one-third more, and perhaps twice as much, garbage as his or her counterparts in the EU and Japan. However, the picture is less clear if we compare amounts of MSW produced per unit of economic productivity. Again, depending on which U.S. data are used, we make either middling or high amounts of trash per unit of GDP, compared with amounts seen in other industrialized nations. By one obvious measure, amount of landfill capacity, we do not make too much trash. This fact is reflected in the price of garbage disposal in the U.S., where rates are far lower than those in other affluent countries. In many nations there is little land to waste, because of high population densities or restrictive land-use policies.

Other indicators for whether we make too much MSW are trends in disposal and recycling rates. Relative to 1960 we appear to make substantially more (73 percent) MSW per capita but much less (31 percent) MSW per unit of GDP. But these statistics are ambiguous, because containers and packaging have become substantially lighter in weight. This trend toward lighter-weight packaging obscures the question of whether we actually throw away less stuff than we did forty years ago. There is no question that Americans recycle much more than they did forty years ago largely because some cities and states have undertaken aggressive recycling programs. Still, the average recycling rate in the U.S. lags behind overall recycling rates in the EU Member States and in Japan.

Recycling and waste-generation practices are seen in the EU and Japan as inseparable from the principles of proximity, pollution prevention, and self-sufficiency. Disposing of trash in a neighboring Member State (in the EU) or prefecture (in Japan) is virtually forbidden, but it is acceptable to transport trash intended for beneficial uses like recycling or waste-to-energy facilities. Various EU directives and Member State laws constrain or forbid landfill disposal of many items found in household trash.

The net result is that, in Japan and in Europe, reducing waste generated is an important goal that serves, and is integrated with, other waste management principles. In contrast, the United States lacks a national integrated MSW management policy and there are no national constraints on trash production and transport. Nor have public officials in Congress or in the executive branch explicitly recognized the possibility that long-distance trash transport might be related to the amount of waste generated.

At the same time, environmental justice issues have surfaced more prominently in U.S. waste management debates than in the EU or Japan. Chapter 3 turns to this aspect of MSW management in the United States.

Costs and Benefits of Interstate Trash Transport

Landfill Capacity, Schools, and Environmental Justice

The number of landfills in the United States has dropped dramatically in recent memory. According to EPA, in 1988 there were almost 8,000 landfills in the United States, but by 2006 that number had decreased to 1,754. The National Solid Waste Management Association estimates that there were 20,000 landfills in the 1970s, dropping to 2,800 in 1995 and remaining at about that level today.[1]

Whatever the exact numbers are, it is evident that many local landfills have closed over the past twenty years. Some of these facilities were environmental nightmares. Fresh Kills Landfill on Staten Island was especially notorious for its enormous size (2,200 acres, occupying 11 percent of Staten Island's total area), noxious odors, air pollution, and for uncontrolled leaks to surrounding waterways. Most of the now-retired landfills were much smaller than Fresh Kills, which was said to be the world's largest operating landfill. In some states—Texas, Alaska, Wisconsin, and Virginia—hundreds of small landfills were shut down.[2]

The high number of closures seemed initially to portend a looming shortfall of landfill capacity that might leave many cities and towns with no place to send their garbage. However, new landfills, many of which are privately operated, tend to be enormous mega-landfills. Landfill operators have found ways of compressing more trash into the same volume. As a result of these techniques and of the relatively large size of recently built landfills, MSW disposal capacity in the United States overall has increased even as the number of landfills has decreased.

Despite the overall national increase in landfill disposal capacity, there are regional variations in number and size of MSW processing facilities. Compare, for example, the MSW disposal capacity of New York with that of Virginia. In 2006, the most recent year for which MSW generation data are readily available, New York State had an estimated population of 19.3 million, and the state's twenty-seven landfills accepted 7.8 million tons of waste. Projected overall capacity was 151 million tons, which means that at current disposal rates New York's landfills should last for approximately nineteen more years, or until 2025. New York also has ten waste-to-energy facilities that in 2006 processed 3.7 million tons of MSW. Of course, these units do not strictly "dispose" of MSW, in that the ash from these units must be recycled or dumped in landfills.

In contrast, Virginia's 2006 estimated population is 7.6 million, which means that there are 2.5 New Yorkers for every Virginian. But in 2006 Virginia managed 16.9 million tons of MSW, or 47 percent more than was managed in New York. Of the MSW managed in Virginia in 2006, 2.1 million tons was incinerated first and 14.8 million tons was disposed of in fifty-seven landfills whose total projected capacity in 2006 was 257 million tons. This means that the annual rate of trash landfilled per capita in Virginia was 1.95 tons per resident, more than four times that in New York, where the annual per capita disposal rate was 0.4 tons per resident. Remaining MSW capacity in Virginia amounts to 33.8 tons per resident, while that in New York State is 7.8 tons per resident. At current disposal rates, Virginia's huge MSW landfill capacity would be consumed by 2023. The Virginia Department of Environmental Quality estimates that 10,000 acres (or about 15 square miles) in Virginia have been permitted as landfills, an area that is slightly larger than the entire city of Charlottesville, Virginia (which covers 10 square miles).[3]

These contrasting MSW profiles lead to the question of why communities in Virginia are more likely to accept mega-landfills in their midst than are communities in New York State. Sheer amount of land area cannot explain this difference, as New York has 54,555 square miles as compared with 42,774 square miles in Virginia. The answer to this question must be found in politics, economics, geography, or a combination thereof.

In the following section I discuss the socioeconomic characteristics of landfill communities in Virginia and in selected other states as well. In so doing, I rely on statistical reports generated through other studies. I end the chapter by describing different conceptual ways of defining "environmental justice."

BENEFITS AND BURDENS OF MUNICIPAL SOLID WASTE

Municipal solid waste has traditionally been a liability to cities and towns. It became even more problematic as urban areas grew denser and as Progressive Era urban reformers came to regard trash as a health problem and, eventually, as a source of environmental pollution.

Municipalities have employed a variety of disposal techniques over time, including pig farming, ocean or lake dumping, and land disposal. Incinerators have been used since the late nineteenth century to transform trash into air pollution and ash, which is then buried in landfills. For a time, incineration was especially heavily used in places like New York City. According to one accounting, there were more than seven hundred garbage incinerators in the United States in the late 1930s, as opposed to approximately one hundred now.[4]

Perhaps because the United States has a generous amount of land, dumping or landfilling has always been a widely used disposal technique. Urban managers tended in the late nineteenth and early twentieth centuries to dispose of trash in small dumps distributed across their cities. For example, in 1917 Cleveland owned twenty-five dumps and there were many privately owned landfills in the city as well. Until the "sanitary" landfill came into widespread use after World War II, dumps tended to be just that: places where garbage was spilled onto the ground in concentrated, stinking piles that crawled with vermin. Sanitary landfills improved on dumps in that trash was placed in trenches and then it was compacted and covered daily with soil. The first such landfill was developed in Fresno, California, in 1937.[5]

A microcosm of the country's shifting patterns of waste disposal is found in Chicago, where we see patterns typical of those in urban areas across the nation. In the nineteenth century, trash mixed with industrial waste was used to fill wetlands, enabling development and raising the level of the city. Some areas of Chicago rest on a dozen feet of waste. In one of the most dramatic uses of solid waste for landfilling, the City used debris from its massive 1871 fire to create new landscapes where none had existed before. Land "reclamation," which involves the use of garbage and industrial wastes to fill wet areas, formed solid ground for many lakefront properties, including Grant Park.

Eventually, public protests caused the shutdown of landfills and dumps located within the City's limits. By 1963 the City was sending its trash to seventy-two suburban landfills. From the 1950s through the mid-1990s Chicago also relied on incineration as the City encountered increasing difficulty in finding suitable dumping grounds for its trash. However, as documented in David Pellow's book *Garbage Wars,* Chicago's MSW incinerators attracted controversy because of pollution and environmental justice concerns. In 1984 Mayor Harold Washington and the Chicago City Council established a moratorium on new landfills within the City's limits and in 1996 the infamous Northwest Incinerator closed. As of 2000, fourteen huge suburban landfills served Chicago and surrounding counties.[6]

In effect, Chicago's trash has been pushed over time from within the City's limits outward into large suburban landfills. Some inactive landfills are among Chicago's 240 Superfund sites, although many landfills have been converted over time into recreational sites. It was in the Chicago suburb of Oakwood that a small company named Waste Management, Inc. was incorporated in 1968. Waste Management is now one of the dominant national waste management companies.[7]

Virginia's recent history of MSW management reproduces some of the same trends seen in Chicago at a larger geographic scale. According to a historical review completed in 1998 by the Virginia Department of Environmental Quality, hundreds of landfills became inactive or were closed during the 1960s and 1970s. Between approximately 1975 and 1995 another two hundred landfills stopped accepting waste and were closed or became "inactive," meaning that they are in the process of being closed. Most of these closed or inactive landfills were less than 100 acres in size, which is relatively small by today's standards. Figure 5

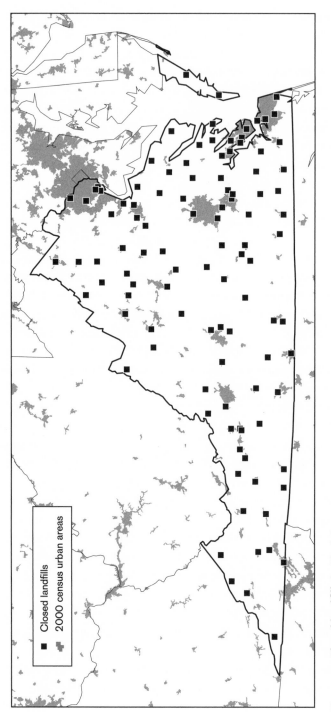

FIGURE 5. Closed landfills in Virginia.

shows the locations of closed MSW landfills in Virginia for which geographic information is readily available.

Fifty-seven operating MSW landfills remain in Virginia. Virginia's open MSW landfills with readily available geographic information are shown in figure 6. Each of the largest landfills extends across several hundred acres and accepts trash from within the state and from outside the state. Most of these facilities are operated by private companies, and because they accept trash from hundreds of miles away, they are called regional or "mega" landfills. The term "mega-landfill" has no formal definition, but it is used here to designate landfills whose total capacity exceeds ten million tons or that accepted greater than 2 percent of MSW disposed in Virginia in 2007. By this definition, Virginia is home to fifteen mega-landfills. Eighty percent of MSW disposed in Virginia in 2007 went to one of the fifteen mega-landfills shown in figure 6.

Figure 5 shows that MSW disposal was formerly scattered much more widely around the state. As shown in figures 6 and 7, MSW disposal is now concentrated in the central to southeastern quadrant of the state, where ten mega-landfills that are predominantly located in rural areas together account for 54 percent of the state's remaining MSW landfill disposal capacity. In 2007, 9.2 million tons were managed at these same ten mega-landfills, which represents 68 percent of all MSW disposed at landfills in Virginia.[8]

To put these figures into perspective, in 2007 Virginia's population of 7.7 million generated about 10.3 million tons of MSW. This means that the ten mega-landfills concentrated in Virginia's central to southeastern quadrant managed an amount of MSW equal to 90 percent of that generated by the Commonwealth's entire population. Virginia's population is increasingly concentrated in the northern part of the state, where one of every three Virginians resides. In contrast, only 758,600 people—10 percent of Virginia's population—reside in the counties hosting these ten mega-landfills. This means that the MSW disposal rate per capita for the areas hosting the ten mega-landfills was 12.1 tons/capita, which was six times the 2006 average per capita landfill disposal rate in Virginia as a whole, and thirty times the 2006 average disposal rate per capita in New York State.[9]

These figures illustrate perhaps more clearly than any others the recent trend toward concentration of waste disposal in the United States,

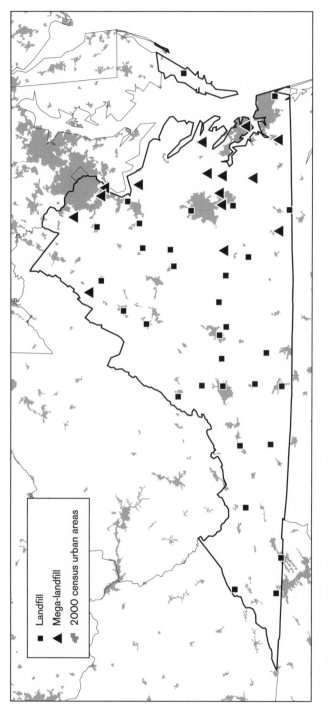

FIGURE 6. Open landfills and mega-landfills in Virginia.

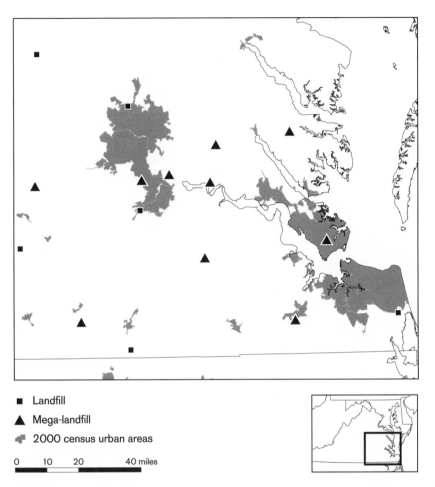

FIGURE 7. Open landfills and mega-landfills in central to southeastern Virginia.

which has its roots in a variety of factors. In the past fifteen years many large cities (like New York City, the District of Columbia, and Chicago), and many smaller towns as well (like Charlottesville, home to the University of Virginia), have chosen to contract with private waste management firms rather than open new, publicly owned landfills or bring old ones up to stricter EPA and state environmental standards. Modern facilities are more expensive to operate, and the economies of scale favor large landfills over smaller ones. The Supreme Court's 1994 *Carbone v. Clarkstown* decision compounded local governments' conundrum over whether to keep trash at home in new, modern facilities or to send it elsewhere. The *Carbone* decision limited local governments in their ability to direct trash to local facilities, thereby making it difficult to ensure a steady stream of revenue that would support modern MSW management.

I came to understand this dilemma firsthand. A Charlottesville, Virginia, task force to which I was appointed in 1996 struggled over many months of meetings to decide whether to close the decades-old rural landfill or open new, environmentally protective cells (landfill sections) in the same location. Ultimately, local authorities decided to close the local landfill and to contract for disposal elsewhere. Charlottesville's MSW is now disposed of in a nearby regional landfill.[10]

Perhaps the most conspicuous and publicly contentious closure decision in the United States to date involved the Fresh Kills Landfill on Staten Island. In 2001 New York City closed Fresh Kills, which at 2,200 acres was almost three times the size of Central Park. Built in 1948, Fresh Kills came into being at a time when marshes and wetlands were considered useless, and even dangerous, because they provided breeding grounds for mosquitoes.[11]

Leslie Allan, a New York City sanitation official, has strenuously defended the decision to send the City's waste elsewhere. Her remarks are quoted here at length since they reflect the justification offered by many local governments exporting MSW.

In exporting its residential waste, the City is exercising nothing more than the right the Constitution extends to cities and states nationwide—responsible, efficient, and environmentally sound solid waste management through heavily regulated and highly competitive private sector businesses. The courts have consistently upheld MSW shipments as a commodity in interstate commerce, and over the years communities have relied on the certainty these decisions provide for protecting long-term, free market plans to manage solid waste. This is especially important in a landscape where the more rigorous environmental protections required under Subtitle D of the Resource and Conservation and Recovery Act (RCRA) have compelled communities to replace old, small landfills with larger, costlier, state-of-the-art, regional facilities that comply with the law. In this context, the right to transport solid waste across state lines complements the basic reality that different regions have varying disposal capacities irrespective of state lines. Areas such as New York City and Chicago, lacking adequate space for landfills and/or prohibited from waste incineration, may be located closer to better and more cost-effective facilities in other states. These facilities need the additional waste generated elsewhere to pay for part of the increased cost of RCRA compliance. . . . For the nation's largest and most densely-populated city of eight million people—comprised of three islands and a peninsula—the ability to send waste to newer, more advanced regional facilities located outside the City's boundaries acknowledges the very environmental, demographic, and geographical realities that made closing Fresh Kills necessary. For the localities that have opted to import our waste, the revenue generated through host fees, licensing fees, and taxes has substantially enhanced the local economy, improved area infrastructure, paid for school construction, paved roads, and assisted host communities in meeting their own waste management needs. Clearly, there are many other jurisdictions nationwide that share New York's approach, since 42 states import and 46 states and Washington, DC, export municipal solid waste.[12]

New York's political leaders would offer further evidence that they seek to act responsibly with respect to their city's trash. In 2004 the City issued a "Request for Expression of Interest" that was intended to solicit in-state proposals for disposal of the City's trash. The City indicated that it was exploring in-state options to redirect the financial benefits of trash disposal to in-state locations and "to reduce the potential for out-of-state jurisdictions to influence the economics or otherwise control the waste disposal infrastructure upon which the City depends." The 2006 solid waste plan for the City pledged enhanced investment in recycling operations to increase the City's overall recycling rate to 25 percent in 2007. The plan calls for transfer stations to be located at the waterfront in each borough, thereby spreading the trash burden across the City's residents instead of concentrating it in Brooklyn and the Bronx, which in 2004 together handled 73 percent of the city's solid waste. Trains and barges will carry the waste to its disposal sites, reducing the traffic and pollution created by truck transport. According to Senator Hillary Rodham Clinton, New York State and New York City will send trash only to sites that have signed legally binding host community agreements that signify their willingness to accept out-of-state waste.[13]

Although many cities and towns have eliminated local landfills, waste management firms have found other communities willing to accept new, privately operated landfills in exchange for trash disposal services and host community fees. Those fees are often assessed on a per-ton basis, so that the more trash managed, the more revenue is generated for host communities. Some of these towns and cities are rural and they are thus strapped for property tax revenues.

Thomas Woodham, then vice-chair of the Lee County, South Carolina, Council, testified in 2003 hearings before the U.S. House of Representatives that landfill revenues comprise 21 percent of the county's local budget and that local trash is dumped for free at the regional private landfill. Lee County has also saved almost $2 million in landfill closure costs, presumably because they were assumed by the new landfill's operator. Methane emitted at the new facility is being used to generate electricity. As measured by household income, the County is the poorest in South Carolina, with a median income of $13,896. Lee County has a much greater percentage of African Americans (62.9 percent) than does the state as a whole (29.4 percent).[14]

Additional examples of host fees illustrate their powerful attraction to economically vulnerable rural or small-town communities. In 1995 officials in Perry County, Illinois, whose 2005 population was 22,815, approved a new, privately operated landfill, transfer, and recycling operation that would add 10 percent to the state's overall landfill capacity and an estimated twenty-three years' worth of landfill capacity to southern Illinois. In exchange, the County expects to receive $500,000 to $1 million a year when the landfill reaches its full daily limit of two thousand tons.

Charles City County, Virginia, has been the site of a 600-acre mega-landfill since 1990. In 1997 the County collected $4.5 million in fees, which at that time sufficed to cover the debt on three new schools and allowed officials to reduce the property tax rate by 44 percent. In 2007 Charles City County collected $8.2 million in host fees from Waste Management. Charles City County is rural, with a 2006 population estimated at 7,221, and the County's 2004 median household income was $44,887 as compared with $51,103 in Virginia as a whole. The landfill's revenues clearly make a palpable difference for the schools in this sparsely populated county. Academic studies confirm the anecdotal intuition that higher levels of spending on teaching resources make a difference. A formal study of the variation in Virginia school district expenditures on teaching found that higher spending translated into better student outcomes, at least for some measures.[15]

Despite the prospect of millions of dollars in annual host fees, not all communities can be enticed to accept landfills. For example, a pair of neighboring but economically different towns in Massachusetts both rejected waste disposal facilities in their communities. In 2004 East Bridgewater, Massachusetts, rejected overwhelmingly a landfill expansion proposed by Browning Ferris Industries that would have brought an estimated $29 million in revenue and services over seven years. This small New England town has only 8,230 registered voters, but the town meeting on the subject of the landfill attracted 1,800 of the town's residents, highlighting the intensity of the community's response. Unlike Lee County, South Carolina, and Charles City, Virginia, the most recent median household income available for East Bridgewater of $60,311 (for 1999) exceeded that of the state's overall median income of $50,502 for that same year. Residents of less-affluent Brockton, Massachusetts, also objected to BFI's proposal, because they feared they would be adversely affected by a landfill expansion in nearby East Bridgewater. Brockton's 1999 median household income of $39,507 was substantially lower than that for the state overall.[16]

No county or city can be forced to accept a privately owned and operated waste disposal site. Those who choose to host such sites receive needed revenue that, in more-affluent, more densely populated jurisdictions, would probably flow from property taxes generated by homes. Tax revenues are the proximate reason that many rural areas accept landfills, and in so doing they also gain easy access to a new disposal site. In the wake of the 1994 *Carbone v. Clarkstown* Supreme Court decision, it became riskier for public entities to undertake the building and financing of a new, expensive, environmentally modern waste disposal facility. When the financing of schools and other public services depends heavily on property values and when publicly owned disposal facilities cannot be assured of enough trash revenue to stay financially viable, many rural areas have invited privately operated mega-landfills into their midst.

Waste management companies tend to gravitate toward regions that will help them minimize costs. Attractive locations would be near major transportation corridors like interstate highways, rail lines, or major rivers and they would likely feature relatively inexpensive land. Densely populated areas would present obvious logistical challenges for siting landfills and would likely mean more-intense "Not-in-my-back-yard" (NIMBY) opposition. The generalized result of these various forces has been to push trash disposal facilities away from urban areas to far-flung, sparsely populated communities who willingly accept trash for cash.

Specific characteristics of Virginia's southeastern rural communities and Virginia's regulations for MSW facilities may have attracted waste management firms. Southeast Virginia has favorable topography for landfills in the form of reasonably flat open spaces. One report sponsored by the Virginia General Assembly speculated that "minimal zoning requirements" typify the southern portion of the state. Virginia's regulations for the operation of MSW landfills are less stringent than those in New York State along several important lines, including liner requirements, amount of compacted soil for intermediate covers, leachate management, groundwater monitoring systems, and groundwater sampling. However, some MSW landfills in Virginia exceed state regulatory requirements.[17]

In the most recent national survey of landfill tipping fees, which are the charge per ton levied on waste, rates were 53 percent higher in the Northeast Region, which includes New York State, than they were in the Mid-Atlantic Region, which includes Virginia, an outcome that undoubtedly reflects higher costs of operation in the Northeast. Among these costs are property taxes. Real estate taxes are famously high in New York State generally, prompting the recent formation of a property tax Commission and a 2008 proposal by Governor Paterson to cap local property taxes. In Virginia the average property tax rate is lower than the national average.[18]

Race, Income, and Solid Waste

When the first major U.S. environmental laws were enacted in the 1970s, the term "environmental justice" had not been coined and there is little evidence that the underlying concepts were recognized by members of the environmental community. Politicians and environmental advocates in that period seemed not to contemplate the possibility that pollution and undesirable land uses disproportionately affect people of color and low income. It would take several pioneering studies in the 1980s to bring the terms "environmental racism" and "environmental justice" and their associated concepts into environmental policy discourse. Since then, a rich literature has developed in which scholars, practitioners, and environmental justice advocates have explored to what extent environmental hazards disproportionately burden the poor and non-whites.

The environmental justice movement in the United States was launched around the issue of hazardous waste landfills. Two seminal studies published in the 1980s concluded that hazardous waste sites in the South were located disproportionately in minority communities. At the behest of Congressional Delegate Walter Fauntroy, the U.S. General Accounting Office (GAO) studied the location of hazardous waste landfills in EPA's Region IV, which encompasses several states in the South. The GAO concluded that three of these four sites were located in communities with higher proportions of minorities than their proportion statewide.[19]

In a follow-up study, NYU School of Law Professor Vicki Been concluded that the communities studied in the GAO report were disproportionately minority at the time the waste sites were built and that, therefore, the siting process in these cases unjustly affected minorities. In a 1987 study that analyzed hazardous waste site locations by zip code across the United States, the United Church of Christ Commission for Racial Justice found that communities with hazardous waste sites tended to have more minorities than those lacking such sites, and that the percentage of minorities in a given zip code increased with the number of hazardous waste sites. The Commission's executive director, Benjamin Chavis, adopted the label "environmental racism" to describe the phenomenon documented in these various reports.[20]

Municipal waste landfill siting has been studied too. Robert Bullard's *Dumping in Dixie* describes the location of MSW landfills and incinerators in Houston, Texas. According to Bullard's data, in the early 1980s most of Houston's MSW incinerators and all of its MSW landfills were located in disproportionately black neighborhoods. A re-analysis of these same sites by Vicki Been found that siting decisions and "market dynamics" both had disproportionate effects on African Americans and the poor. What Been means by "market dynamics" is that property values dropped in most areas surrounding Houston landfills and those same areas then became even poorer and more African American than they were prior to the building of the MSW facilities.[21]

The GAO has attempted to discover to what extent disproportionate siting of MSW landfills is a pattern repeated across the nation. The GAO's 1995 study of 292 MSW landfills nationwide found little evidence of widespread disproportionate effects by class or race. The percentage of minorities living within one mile of landfills in urban and non-metropolitan areas tended to be lower than that in the rest of the surrounding county. GAO estimated that the percentage of minorities living within one mile of landfills was higher than the percentage of minorities living in the rest of the county only 27 percent of the time. In many cases in which more minorities lived within the one-mile radius relative to the rest of the county, GAO found that the differences between those percentages were quite small. For only 13 percent of the metropolitan landfills and 9 percent of the non-metropolitan landfills did the percentage of minorities within one mile of the landfills exceed the percentage outside the radius by at least 10 percent.

GAO also found no evidence that the presence of groundwater contamination, monitoring systems, or liners was correlated with the percentage of minorities living nearby. In fact, non-metropolitan landfills with higher percentages of minorities living nearby relative to the rest of the county were more likely to have groundwater monitoring systems than were landfills with higher percentages of non-minorities living within one mile. For both metropolitan and non-metropolitan landfills, people living within one mile of the landfill were equally likely to have higher and lower median household incomes than people in the rest of the county as a whole. However, when compared with the national average income as opposed to that in the surrounding county, people living near 65 percent of the non-metropolitan landfills showed median household incomes lower than the national average. This same pattern was not repeated for metropolitan landfills.[22]

The GAO study, while comprehensive, did not distinguish between landfills based on their size or age. Even though recently built mega-landfills must install more environmental controls than the smaller, leaky landfills that have closed in droves over the past twenty years, mega-landfills have the potential to cause huge impacts on surrounding communities now and in the future by virtue of their size. This very issue was the focus of interest to members of the Virginia General Assembly, who were concerned about the demographic characteristics of communities near eight new regional MSW landfills.

This concern prompted a 1994 study by the General Assembly's Joint Legislative Audit and Review Commission (JLARC) that examined the race and income characteristics of communities surrounding all existing or planned MSW facilities in Virginia. The JLARC study found that the counties with eight private regional landfills (or mega-landfills) sited or permitted since 1988 were not only rural, they were poorer and had a higher minority population rate than the state as a whole. Specifically, these counties had a median 1990 per capita income of $17,095, as opposed to the median statewide income of $19,701. Median housing value in these same counties was $55,600, as compared with the statewide value of $91,000, and 37 percent of the landfill county residents were minorities, as compared with a statewide figure of 22 percent. In 2006 Charles City County, Virginia, which was mentioned above and which is home to one such mega-landfill, had a black population of 46.4 percent, as compared with 19.9 percent in the state as a whole.[23]

When the JLARC analysts examined community characteristics within one, two, and three miles of the same eight Virginia mega-landfills, the study's results did not change: at these radii the proportion of minorities was 42 percent, 48 percent, and 40 percent, respectively. Thirty-five percent of the proposed or already sited MSW facilities in Virginia were located in communities whose minority population exceeded by at least 5 percent that of the overall county. In half of these cases the difference between these two percentages exceeded 20 percent. Discriminatory effects were also found when state enforcement actions were examined: "facilities located in predominantly minority communities tended to be inspected less frequently and have longer periods of noncompliance."[24]

Of course, in return for accepting huge amounts of waste for dumping in their jurisdictions, the counties in which these regional landfills were located received virtually free waste disposal and substantial revenues. In 1994–95 the average revenue received in counties hosting private regional landfills was $1.5 million, which constituted 10 percent of these areas' average total local revenue of $11 million. Average local revenue in counties without regional landfills was at least three times higher because of their ability to generate substantial property tax revenues.[25]

By contrast with the JLARC study, a comparable study performed in Massachusetts found no evidence of class or racial bias in the location of MSW landfills. Faber and Krieg found extensive evidence that many kinds of facilities posing environmental risks were disproportionately located in low-income and/or minority Massachusetts towns, with the exception of the state's 566 MSW landfills, which were present in "91.3 percent of communities, making them relatively constant across all communities." Recent census figures show that East Bridgewater and Brockton, the neighboring Massachusetts towns described above that both opposed an expansion to a local landfill, are quite different from each other and from the overall state demographic profile. Massachusetts as a whole is 84.5 percent white, while East Bridgewater is 98 percent white and Brockton is 61.5 percent white.[26]

Taken as a whole, studies focusing on the location of municipal waste landfills show mixed results. They do not point uniformly toward the conclusion that the poor and minorities invariably, or even usually, suffer disproportionately from pollution-associated trash disposal. However, two important caveats must be kept in mind. First, many of these analyses were performed in the late 1980s and early 1990s, before the advent of regional private mega-landfills and at a time when the population of landfills was changing rapidly. Thus, while these analyses reveal important things about the location of landfills before the early 1990s, they are not necessarily descriptive of the situation in the early twenty-first century, which involves many fewer but much larger landfills and more transfer stations, at which MSW is transferred from small local trucks to larger ones for long-distance transport to distant disposal facilities. A 2000 study conducted by the Environmental Justice Advisory Council, a working group that advises the EPA, found that waste transfer stations in New York City and in Washington, D.C., are clustered in poor and minority neighborhoods.[27]

Second, there are important methodological disputes over the correct methodological approach for environmental justice analytical studies. For example, there is no agreement on whether to use zip codes, neighborhoods, census tracts, or counties as the spatial unit of measurement when describing the population that is affected by a waste disposal facility. Environmental justice scholar Edwardo Rhodes suggests using a variety of spatial units in any given analysis, so as to make the results as robust as possible, and he further suggests comparing the percentage of minority or low-income people in an affected area with those of the next-largest political unit. By this Rhodes means we should compare neighborhood demographic statistics with those of the surrounding county, rather than with the state as a whole, to determine if the neighborhood affected by a landfill displays a different demographic profile from unaffected areas.[28]

The Virginia JLARC study remains one of the few studies to have compared income and race statistics at the neighborhood, county, and state levels. Thus, this analysis must be regarded as especially convincing. While it is unclear whether minorities and the less affluent are burdened with more landfills in the United States as a whole, the evidence in Virginia points to the conclusion that private mega-landfills are sited in disproportionately black, low-income areas. A recent, informal look indicates that the ten counties hosting mega-landfills in the central to southeastern quadrant of Virginia are poorer (median income is $44,525, as opposed to $51,103 statewide) and less white (59.57 percent white, as opposed to 73.3 percent statewide) than Virginia as a whole. This analysis suggests that the patterns described in the JLARC study are still realized today, but this updated work does not describe the demographic profiles of the communities immediately surrounding the landfills, and thus it is less conclusive than the JLARC study.[29]

These studies with their varied results lead naturally to two questions: (1) Is it unjust for landfills to be located in communities that are vulnerable politically and economically by virtue of their low population density, high percentage of minorities, or relatively low income, even if those communities receive seemingly generous compensation? And (2), if the answer to the first question is "yes," what remedies should be employed? The final section of this chapter explores these two questions.

INFORMATION, VOICE, AND CONSENT

A host of empirical studies performed by academics, think-tank scholars, and government agencies have claimed that, in many instances, the poor and people of color disproportionately bear the burden of waste facilities. But informed observers disagree on the extent of these inequities. Political scientist Christopher Foreman concludes after scrutinizing the literature that "even a reasonably generous reading of the foundational empirical research alleging environmental inequity along racial lines must leave room for profound skepticism regarding the reported results. Taken as a whole this research offers, at best, only tenuous support for the hypothesis of racial inequity in siting or exposure, and no insight into the crucial issues of risk and health impact." For example, Foreman cites scientific studies contradicting the conclusion that residents of the Lower Mississippi River, who live near a concentrated collection of refineries and chemical factories, suffer excessive levels of cancer. John Hird found that counties with minority percentages exceeding the national average were more likely to have Superfund sites, but that more-affluent counties had more sites. Evan Ringquist examined all civil penalties in federal district court (a total of more than a thousand cases) between 1974 and 1991 under the federal Clean Air Act, Clean Water Act, and Resource Conservation and Recovery Act and found no evidence of racial or income bias in fines assessed. Vicki Been agrees with the observation that disproportionate outcomes exist, but she has asserted that they can result from two very different kinds of processes: either siting in disproportionately black or poor neighborhoods, or demographic changes brought about by increased industrial activity.[30]

Other observers point to evidence that in many places across the United States minorities and the poor experience higher exposures to contaminants from a wide variety of sources, including (but not limited to) urban air pollution, solid waste facilities, and chemical factories. Some of this evidence with respect to solid waste facilities was described earlier in this chapter. Blood lead levels associated with learning disabilities have been found in children who are African American, Mexican American, low-income, who reside in urban areas exceeding one million population, or who live in older housing. EPA's phase-out of leaded gasoline has helped to lower blood lead levels across all groups in the U.S. Environmental historian Andrew Hurley shows that between 1945 and 1980 low-income and minority residents of Gary, Indiana, suffered more than their affluent white counterparts from environmental contamination associated with waste dumping and land-use decisions. Chris Foreman asserts that farmworker exposure to pesticides is alarmingly high and that this issue should be elevated as a public health priority. David Pellow documents the alarming number of waste facilities located in poor African American neighborhoods in Chicago. Robert Bullard undertook pioneering empirical work on landfills in Houston and toxic exposures in the American South. While his analyses have been criticized, his relentless focus on environmental racism has forced environmental policymakers to confront policy problems that were previously ignored.[31]

Although the empirical literature does not permit sweeping generalizations to be made about the extent to which the poor and minorities suffer disproportionate exposure to pollution and its attendant risks, the affluent can more readily isolate themselves from solid waste sites and from many types of pollution because they have more power to decide where they will live. People of means can use their financial and political resources to resist having sources of pollution move into their neighborhoods. Geographer and environmental justice scholar Laura Pulido terms this phenomenon "white privilege," which she defines as the "privileges and benefits that accrue to white people by virtue of their whiteness."

In a sense, Pulido's theoretical construct trumps questions about the extent and causes of environmentally unjust outcomes. She is saying, in essence, that the affluent and politically connected, who historically have been disproportionately white in the United States, use their economic and political clout to avoid or block development that is perceived as undesirable. Those who have less clout, less mobility, and fewer economic development possibilities thus often find themselves living near to the landfills or to other undesirable land uses. Alternatively, the disenfranchised (such as Native Americans or Hispanos) may find that they cannot use public lands for grazing or invite landfills onto their land because of opposition from more-powerful neighbors. The Campo Indian tribe in San Diego County encountered intense political resistance to their proposal to site an MSW landfill on their reservation, to the point that the landfill company eventually withdrew its proposal.[32]

Much as environmental justice scholarship is divided, the normative literature is also far from unanimous with respect to the questions of whether disproportionate burdens are always unfair and how they should be remedied. Depending on one's point of view, unequal distribution of pollution is perfectly justifiable, sometimes justifiable, or never justifiable. Of course, even those who oppose any inequities in the distribution of pollution would not argue that it makes sense to build landfills in every U.S. county or city, because we know that some soils and topographic conditions are wholly unsuitable. For example, areas with permeable soils through which landfill liquids leak quickly, with high groundwater or nearby surface waters, with fractured bedrock, or with mountainous terrain do not provide optimal circumstances for landfills. But even after eliminating sites with physically unsuitable characteristics, there remain many possible locations for landfills or incinerators in the United States, leaving much room for arguments over where they should go.

There are a variety of opinions on when—if ever—it is morally acceptable to expose people to unequal concentrations of pollution or polluting sources. Not surprisingly, various federal laws embody contradictory notions of fairness with respect to environmental quality. For example, if we examine two essential provisions of the federal Clean Air Act, we find different answers to the question, should every person have the right to clean air? Congress answered this question affirmatively when it created the National Ambient Air Quality Standards (NAAQS) program. The NAAQS are uniform standards nationwide for acceptable levels of six major pollutants—ozone (smog), fine particulate matter, lead, sulfur dioxide, nitrogen dioxide, and carbon monoxide; the standards are determined by EPA so as to protect public health with a margin of safety. From the inception of the NAAQS program, the Clean Air Act's goal has been to bring every area in the country into attainment with the NAAQS. Despite the fact that much remains to be done to achieve this mark, the ethical underpinning of this program is that no one should be exposed to unhealthful air quality, no matter what the cost. That is, equity should take priority over economic efficiency.

In contrast, the "cap-and-trade" acid rain provisions of the Clean Air Act accept disparate levels of air pollution in different geographic areas of the country. Under these provisions, national, statewide, or regional emissions caps are set for sulfur dioxide and nitrogen oxides emissions from power plants. The philosophy behind this regulatory approach is that as long as the overall caps are reached, sources should be allowed to trade allowances as their individual economic circumstances dictate.

Affected sources may buy or sell pollution rights to ensure that they have enough allowances to cover their emissions. Unequal deposition and air concentrations are an inevitable and expected consequence of this approach. Cap-and-trade programs elevate economic efficiency over fairness, although the existence of the emission caps makes it likely that most areas of the country will experience some emission reductions.

Along similar lines, we can distinguish among normative environmental justice scholars according to whether they are willing to sanction inequitable distribution of pollution and, if so, under what circumstances. On the one hand, there are those who advocate equally clean environments for all. Longtime environmental justice activist and scholar Robert Bullard advocates pollution standards that will provide equal protection, much as civil rights legislation guarantees legal protection from discrimination. Specifically, he asserts that "the solution to environmental injustice lies in the realm of equal protection of all individuals, groups and communities. No community, rich or poor, urban or suburban, black or white, should be allowed to become a 'sacrifice zone' or the dumping ground."[33]

Standing at the opposite end of the philosophical spectrum from Bullard is economist Larry Summers, who, as the World Bank's chief economist, infamously articulated the view that inequities in pollution are highly rational and even desirable. In a brief memo that was published in *The Economist* and was immediately circulated widely, Summers said that sending pollution to developing countries from developed countries makes eminent sense because in developing areas the monetized social benefits of additional pollution are more likely to outweigh the attendant social costs.[34]

Summers did not extend his logic to the long-distance transport of pollution within the United States. However, many economists might see a similar defensible logic in sending trash to areas where it is cheaper to build landfills and where the willingness to accept landfills is higher than it is, for example, in upstate New York. In the economist's view, it makes no sense to "equalize" exposure to landfills, because to do so would mean forcing landfills into areas with higher construction and management costs. According to this rationale, as long as all new landfills are required to have modern environmental controls, society is better off if they are sited in places where they cost less to construct and operate and where fewer people would be exposed to releases of pollution. In this line of argument, the waste market is responding appropriately to environmental and economic concerns by moving us away from many, problematic landfills located in densely populated urban centers and toward fewer, better-protected ones in rural areas. And the communities who host the landfills gain compensation and cheap waste disposal.

These two positions reflect different ideas about the definition of environmental racism and about whether landfill host communities are more appropriately viewed as social victims or as economic agents. On the one hand is the claim that disproportionate landfill siting is attributable to institutionalized racism and an unfettered trash market that combine to victimize people of color. According to this view, the powerful dominate the less powerful politically, via the NIMBYism that keeps MSW facilities out of affluent areas, and also economically, by providing vulnerable communities with few resources to resist the technical claims and financial inducements of MSW companies. On the other hand is the view that by taking advantage of the MSW market, landfill host communities become positive, empowered agents of their own economic development. In this perspective, questioning their decisions to accept MSW landfills amounts to environmental paternalism that is a form of political oppression.

Some environmental justice scholars have adopted normative principles that, somewhat paradoxically, adopt elements from both of these positions. The policy prescriptions flowing from these principles recognize the impracticality and excessive cost of having every U.S. city or town run its own waste disposal facility, while rejecting a situation in which the more affluent dump willy-nilly on the less affluent. Such solutions attempt to empower vulnerable communities politically and economically so that they are better able to ask appropriate questions, ensure the highest level of ongoing environmental protection, demand suitable compensation, or resist landfills entirely.

Included in this school of thought is Kristin Shrader-Frechette, who asserts that those who are asked to bear disproportionate risks must be able to give free, informed consent in order for those burdens to be fairly imposed. In her view, risks are imposed fairly only when all of the following conditions have been met: risks have been fully disclosed to host communities; the members of those communities have fully understood those risks; they have voluntarily consented to the imposition of those risks; and, they are competent enough to give "autonomous authorization."[35] These conditions presume that members of communities asked to host regional landfills might well be confused by the technical information presented to them about potential health and environmental risks. Residents of poor rural areas are also unlikely to be in a position to give full voluntary consent, since they are often desperate for tax revenue, jobs, or an inexpensive place to dispose of their trash.

Free, informed consent as envisioned by Shrader-Frechette requires thorough, repeated public vetting of the potential for waste facilities to contaminate water and air now and in the future. She points to memorably incorrect official predictions about leaks at low-level radioactive waste facilities that underestimated the potential for off-site contamination by several orders of magnitude. Her observations underscore the need to ensure that host communities have the ability to evaluate expert opinions. This means imparting technical information in ordinary, layperson's language and, potentially, appointing outside experts who could advise those who will be directly affected by a new landfill so that a skeptical, technically informed voice can help guide them in their decision.

These principles also point to the need for a full social and environmental analysis of the effects of regional landfills, including communities affected by garbage transport. Alternative waste management and location options should be considered. Future generations need to be protected and represented, too, as they will suffer from the inevitable leaks of landfills built today. Finally, the host community must be fairly compensated and financial provisions must be made for future contamination that will affect generations to come.

In Shrader-Frechette's view, all of the above-stated conditions must be met before locating a regional landfill in a community that is disproportionately poor or minority. Only then is the outcome fair. In some situations she believes that policymakers should refuse to allow polluting facilities, on the grounds that the affected communities are incapable of granting free, informed consent. In other words, she believes that some people must be protected from bad decisions made under coercive circumstances, for example, when no other viable business opportunities present themselves.[36]

Edwardo Rhodes is among those who believe that, despite the fact that it is infeasible to distribute pollution equally, we must work harder to assure fairer outcomes and procedures. Like Shrader-Frechette, he argues for assuring truly informed consent in order to correct market failure. Rhodes believes that the solid waste market is malfunctioning in that those most affected by landfills are making ill-informed decisions. Thus, their willingness to avoid landfills is inappropriately low. Rhodes predicts that, as members of host communities become better informed about the current and future risks of waste facilities, the costs of locating landfills will increase appropriately.

Rhodes embraces EPA's definition of environmental justice, which strives for "fair and meaningful involvement" by people of all incomes and ethnicities, the "same degree of protection from environmental and health hazards," and "equal access to decision-making processes." Fair treatment does not imply equal outcomes; rather, "equal distribution of negative or positive consequences implies perfectly homogeneous preferences and circumstances, which have no validity in the real world. . . . Disproportionate effects . . . are unfair only when they result from a lack of political or economic power, as opposed to resulting from well-informed free choice." In this framework the federal government must take a forceful role in evaluating relative risks and in communicating them clearly to affected communities, so that the people in those areas can make better decisions about whether to accept landfills and, if so, how much compensation they deserve. Rhodes opposes paternalistic governmental decisions that deny communities their own voice on the grounds of avoiding economic exploitation. He believes that this is a misappropriation of power.[37]

Empowerment is a goal that Christopher Foreman also espouses, but he wants to give minority communities information about the many sources of risk in their lives so that they can choose which hazards to attack first. He worries that advocates of environmental justice distract minorities from the much larger health risks posed by obesity and smoking. "Anyone living in a big city," Foreman writes, "is likely breathing dirtier air than anyone living elsewhere."[38] While he does not dismiss the need for attentiveness to environmental hazards in minority and poor communities, Foreman emphasizes the need for members of such communities to take charge of their lives and to manage the risks that they can control, rather than expecting the government to produce health and wealth.

In essence, Foreman, Shrader-Frechette, and Rhodes all emphasize the related goals of economic and political empowerment of communities that are potential or actual landfill hosts. Foreman emphasizes the broad goal of creating livable, healthy communities, and he warns against "flexing of advocacy muscle" that might distract from other, more important health-related issues. Shrader-Frechette and Rhodes want to ensure that ordinary people can understand fully the environmental implications of hosting landfills or other types of solid waste facilities. Discussions around landfills and their environmental impacts are necessarily loaded with technical jargon that can be intimidating and that often papers over important uncertainties. For example, it is often very difficult or even impossible to know whether landfill leaks might penetrate the substrate and thereby contaminate groundwater or surface waters. Outside experts can translate technical documents into laymen's terms so that their meaning is transparent to members of the general public. In this way, ordinary citizens can appreciate the uncertainties embedded in expert pronouncements.

To Rhodes and Shrader-Frechette, genuine political empowerment should be complemented by fair economic compensation for present and future generations. Poor communities should not be forced to accept less by way of compensation than better-off communities. Future generations must be provided for as well.

Lessons from the Environmental Justice Literature

The environmental justice literature helps us recognize that part of the problem with interstate trash transport is that at least in Virginia, and perhaps elsewhere, low-income, sparsely populated communities are accepting waste from better-off, more densely populated communities. Crucial questions include whether host communities are compensated sufficiently and whether ordinary citizens are receiving full, comprehensible, and impartial environmental information, not only while facilities are under consideration but also while they are operating.

On the one hand, it is a good thing that the many old, environmentally uncontrolled landfills that once dotted our landscape have closed and that new municipal waste landfills must contain and control their air and water pollution. Trash now moves across state lines in part because these old landfills have closed, and in part because new, more environmentally protective landfills are more expensive to site and operate. These are natural and desirable outcomes from a new, more environmentally protective regulatory regime.

However, even if deliberate discrimination cannot be proven, it is still unjust to dump on vulnerable communities without giving them the opportunity and the means to judge fully the implications of accepting waste facilities. Political and economic differentials help explain why many central and southeastern rural Virginia communities have agreed to host mega-landfills, many of which accept MSW from far-flung places. But as we shall see in the next chapter, our elected representatives in Congress have not explicitly considered this unbalanced playing field of power in their proposals concerning the interstate transport of trash.

CHAPTER 4

Regulatory and Legislative Efforts to Limit the Movement of Trash

It should come as no surprise to learn that municipal governments like to manage where trash goes within their jurisdictions. Garbage presents health hazards and it is aesthetically displeasing. For more than a century municipal authorities have assumed responsibility for ensuring that trash removal takes place, either through public or private trash haulers, and they have also encouraged citizens to stop littering, through public campaigns and the threat of small fines. However, what might prove surprising is the sheer variety of ways in which governments at the state, local, and national level have tried to channel the movement of garbage across their borders.

Efforts to control the flow of trash highlight the "push-me-pull-you" nature of garbage. Dr. Doolittle's mythical creature had two heads, one at either end, and therefore she could not decide which way to go. In similar fashion, garbage's dual nature as both publicly undesirable and commercially valuable has sent it in different, sometimes unpredictable directions depending on the time, place, and circumstances.

This chapter first discusses two opposing kinds of local and/or state actions that have constrained the flow of trash. The first type of action, flow control, restricts the outward movement of garbage collected in a specific area. Using flow control ordinances, cities and towns have forced local trash haulers to deposit their trash in local waste management facilities, partially to recoup the cost of those facilities, many of which were financed by bonds. In the 1994 *Carbone v. Clarkstown* decision the Supreme Court found certain kinds of flow control ordinances invalid. More recent court decisions have upheld local governments that achieve flow control either by using the market to select waste haulers committed to using local facilities or by directing trash to publicly owned facilities. However, the outcome of *Carbone v. Clarkstown* convinced many local governments in the 1990s that they could not afford to finance their own waste management facilities as there was no way to ensure a reliable flow of trash.

An opposite kind of limit attempts to control the inward movement of trash into a state or locality. Such laws have been struck down when courts have decided that they unfairly targeted out-of-state waste. The list of such overturned laws is formidable, starting with the 1978 decision *City of Philadelphia v. New Jersey* (437 U.S. 617 [1978]), and continuing through *Waste Management Holdings, Inc. v. Gilmore* (252 F.3d 316 [4th Cir. 2001]).

Because of court decisions that have increasingly restricted the ability of state or local governments to control the flow of garbage into or out of their jurisdictions, members of Congress have regularly introduced bills that would permit state or local governments to regulate the interstate transport of trash. The last portion of this chapter is devoted to describing the national policy solutions that have been introduced in Congress over the past fifteen years. They include reinstating the right of local government to control the flow of trash into and out of their jurisdictions and permitting state governments to levy extra fees on out-of-state waste. Those proposals have prompted several congressional hearings, and I draw upon the records of those hearings in my description of private- and public-sector reactions to the notion that the Congress should permit constraints on the interstate flow of trash.

State and Local Attempts to Limit the Flow of Trash

The last century of solid waste management in this country shows a distinctive trend toward increasing levels and disparate forms of government control. Since the Progressive Era, when municipalities recognized the need to protect their citizens from trash mounting in the streets, local governments have overseen the related functions of trash collection and disposal.[1] Until the 1970s these efforts were primarily aimed at getting trash away from people and into nearby dumps or incinerators. But in the past thirty years, state and local agencies across the country have gone further in that they have tried increasingly to restrict the flow of trash out of, or into, specific geographic areas. Across the country, state and local governments have enacted ordinances, laws, and taxes whose purpose has been to keep non-local trash out or, alternatively, to prevent trash haulers from removing locally generated garbage to facilities elsewhere because to do so would mean a loss of revenue to local waste management facilities.

Trash flows have varied with market forces and with the variable success of these regulatory efforts. For example, garbage currently moves in vast quantities from New Jersey to Pennsylvania, which remains the state with the highest amounts of imported trash. As befits a member of Congress concerned about his constituents, Senator Arlen Specter of Pennsylvania lists among his environmental priorities reducing the amount of trash imported into his state from, among other places, the neighboring state of New Jersey. But Senator Specter's concern over the burial of New Jersey's garbage in Pennsylvania is historically short-sighted, since trash from Pennsylvania used to travel to New Jersey.[2]

In fact, the first Supreme Court case on the interstate transport of trash was prompted when, in 1973, New Jersey closed its borders to out-of-state trash and the City of Philadelphia sued successfully to overturn that ban. In ruling in Philadelphia's favor, the Supreme Court correctly anticipated the possibility that New Jersey might one day become a trash exporter:

> Today, cities in Pennsylvania and New York find it expedient or necessary to send their waste into New Jersey for disposal, and New Jersey claims the right to close its borders to such traffic. Tomorrow, cities in New Jersey may find it expedient or necessary to send their waste into Pennsylvania or New York for disposal, and those States might then claim the right to close their borders. The Commerce Clause will protect New Jersey in the future, just as it protects her neighbors now, from efforts by one State to isolate itself in the stream of interstate commerce from a problem shared by all.[3]

This case arose because in the 1970s New Jersey had become concerned over its dwindling landfill space. New Jersey also defended its ban on imported trash on the grounds of preventing environmental harm. Justice Rehnquist's dissent, which was also signed by Chief Justice Burger, agreed with this rationale, arguing for the state's right to preserve its natural resources. In a sense, these two justices were arguing for the economists' notion that polluters—in this case, trash exporters like the City of Philadelphia—should be forced to internalize their pollution costs. Citing case precedent, the dissenting justices asserted that trash is a noxious substance against which states may erect a quarantine:

> New Jersey should be free under our past precedents to prohibit the importation of solid waste because of the health and safety problems that such waste poses to its citizens. The fact that New Jersey continues to, and indeed must continue to, dispose of its own solid waste does not mean that New Jersey may not prohibit the importation of even more solid waste into the State. I simply see no way to distinguish solid waste, on the record of this case, from germ infected rags, diseased meat, and other noxious items.[4]

But these views were minority opinions in a string of appellate cases in which the majority overturned state or local solid waste laws because they were judged a form of economic protectionism that unconstitutionally interfered with interstate commerce. Some laws were found to "facially discriminate" against interstate commerce, while others were found to fail the "Pike test," which allows some incidental interference with commerce if there is a genuine local public interest at stake. In the 1978 *City of Philadelphia* decision the Court described its views on the Pike test: "If a legitimate local interest is found then the question becomes one of degree. And the extent of the burden that will be tolerated will of course depend on the nature of the local interest involved, and on whether it could be promoted as well with a lesser impact on interstate activities."[5]

Since deciding *City of Philadelphia,* the Court until quite recently struck down state or local government interference with waste transport. An Alabama tax on out-of-state hazardous waste, a Michigan policy that attempted to conserve landfill capacity, and an Oregon fee on out-of-state garbage were all overturned by the Court. An ardent defender of states' rights, Chief Justice Rehnquist dissented in each case, arguing that the states were merely trying to protect a legitimate health or environmental interest. For example, in *Chemical Waste Management v. Hunt,* Chief Justice Rehnquist asserted that states should have the right to tax scarce commodities like landfill space and that a higher tax for waste generated outside of the state seemed appropriate. In the Michigan case Justices Rehnquist and Blackmun claimed in their minority opinion that states with relatively low population density should have no obligation to accept trash from more-crowded states.[6]

An important Supreme Court decision in this arena is *Carbone v. Clarkstown* (511 U.S. 383 [1994]). To finance its waste management facility the town of Clarkstown, New York, required that all garbage collected within the town must be disposed of at one facility that was operated privately under contract to the town. Carbone, a local trash hauler, shipped some of his trash to a cheaper facility in Indiana and then sued the town. A majority of the Court agreed with Mr. Carbone's case that the flow control ordinance unconstitutionally prevented out-of-state waste management businesses from competing for the town's garbage. Interestingly, the article of commerce was judged to be the processing of waste, not the waste itself.

Justices Rehnquist, Blackmun, and Souter asserted in their dissent that interstate commerce had not been harmed by Clarkstown's actions and that, therefore, the ordinance was constitutional. They regarded this situation as falling under the "market participant exemption" doctrine, by which government authorities may restrict waste movement if they are acting as "proprietors" rather than as regulators. To be considered a "proprietor" a government authority must procure goods or services on the open market. One interpretation of the market participant exemption holds that cities or towns owning their own waste management facilities may engage in practices that favor their own citizens—even flow control.[7]

These cases involve a struggle over who should control the flow of waste. The Assistant District Attorney in Rockland County, New York, claimed that invalidating Clarkstown's ordinance would let the waste industry "ambush" local government efforts to manage waste conscientiously. He argued on behalf of local, environmentally rooted efforts to

support recycling, composting, or waste reduction as opposed to sending trash to a faraway disposal site: "Sound garbage management may
cost more today, but less in the long run (both economically and environmentally) if local citizens are able to choose to solve the problem of
waste proliferation instead of relying on the garbage industry."[8]

On the one hand, flow control represents an effort by local governments to internalize environmental costs and reduce waste rather than
foist locally produced garbage on other communities. But flow control
ordinances can mean higher costs to local consumers who, it has been
argued, are often forced to bear the financial burden of unwise, overly
costly waste management facilities erected by local governments.[9]

Despite the Supreme Court's repeatedly articulated opposition to
state or local laws limiting the flow of trash, state and local governments
have continued to enact them. The Commonwealth of Virginia entered
this political fray when, during the 1990s, the state became the second-
largest importer of trash in the country. In 2007, the latest year for
which data are available, Virginia's landfills and incinerators accepted
15.9 million tons of municipal solid waste, of which 5.6 million tons (or
35 percent of the total) was imported from outside of the state. Sixty-
three percent of imported MSW came from Virginia's neighbors North
Carolina, Maryland, and the District of Columbia, while most of the rest
came from New York and New Jersey, which contributed 28 percent and
6 percent of imported MSW, respectively. New York and New Jersey
contributed only 12 percent of *total* MSW disposed in Virginia in 2007.
Eighty-seven percent of MSW disposed in Virginia in 2007 came from
Virginia or from its immediate neighbors.[10]

Despite the fact that the vast majority of Virginia's MSW originates
within the state or just across its borders, New York City's contribution
has attracted the most attention, and in the late 1990s was the subject of
a public spat between New York City Mayor Rudy Giuliani and Virginia
Governor James Gilmore. Mayor Giuliani inflamed Virginians when he
asserted that New York City and Virginia exist in a "reciprocal" relationship: Virginians enjoy the Big Apple's cultural offerings and financial
institutions, while New Yorkers take advantage of Virginia's landfills.
Outraged responses included that of Jim Spencer, a columnist for the
Newport News Daily Press, who suggested that Virginians barge their
prostitution industry to New York, "in the spirit of letting each place do

what it does best." Governor Gilmore declared, in a letter to Mayor Giuliani, that "The home state of Washington, Jefferson, and Madison has no intention of becoming New York's dumping ground."[11]

Republican Governor Gilmore and the Virginia legislature moved beyond inflamed rhetoric when they enacted in 1999 five new provisions that would have capped the amount of waste allowed in Virginia landfills, prohibited barge transport of trash, and regulated truck transport of trash. Interestingly, even as Governor Gilmore engaged in heated public exchanges with Mayor Giuliani and proclaimed the need to stem the flow of trash deposited in Virginia's landfills, he vetoed a provision enacted by the Virginia General Assembly that would have exacted a modest fee of one to two dollars per ton on all MSW disposed in Virginia's landfills. Gilmore replaced the "Virginia Solid Waste Environmental Stewardship Fund," which would have provided landfill closure grants to local governments, with the "Virginia Landfill Cleanup and Closure Fund," which would serve a similar purpose but would be funded directly by the General Assembly rather than through garbage fees. At the time, Gilmore's appointee as the director of Virginia's Department of Environmental Quality was Dennis Treacy, who had formerly worked for Browning Ferris Industries, a waste management firm. From 1995 to 1998 Gilmore received $100,000 in contributions from the waste management industry.[12]

Observers of Commerce Clause jurisprudence might have predicted that many of the provisions enacted into law would not pass judicial muster because they overtly discriminated against out-of-state MSW. Waste Management, Inc. sued the state, and a federal appeals court overturned the regulations on the grounds that they affected only waste transported from outside the state. Gilmore's successor, Governor Mark Warner, proposed to assess a tax of five dollars per ton on all solid waste landfilled in Virginia, with the monies to be used at the local and state levels for program costs and pollution remediation. That bill failed to pass the Virginia General Assembly, as have recent, more modest versions introduced in the Assembly. It would appear that there is little political will in Virginia for assessing even a small fee on MSW disposal, even if those funds are reserved to remedy the environmental contamination problems that inevitably occur with waste disposal.[13]

Despite the fact that most attempts to constrain the movement of trash have failed in the courts, some efforts have passed judicial muster. In *USA Recycling v. the Town of Babylon* the Second Circuit Court of Appeals upheld Babylon, New York's waste management system that used market incentives to direct the Town's trash to a locally financed incinerator. The Town chose one waste hauler for the entire town through a competitive bidding process and then allowed that hauler to dump trash for free at the local privately owned incinerator whose operators had been guaranteed a certain level of waste by the Town.

The Second Circuit held that Babylon was not discriminating against interstate commerce but, rather, was acting as a market participant in selecting both its hauler and its incinerator operator. Any company, whether in-state or out-of-state, could compete in the Town's waste management market:

> This case boils down to two simple propositions. First, towns can assume exclusive responsibility for the collection and disposal of local garbage. Second, towns can hire private contractors to provide municipal services to residents. In neither case does a town discriminate against, or impose any burden on, interstate commerce. The local interests that are served by consolidating garbage service in the hands of the town—safety, sanitation, reliable garbage service, cheaper service to residents—would in any event outweigh any arguable burdens placed on interstate commerce.[14]

In 2007 the Supreme Court affirmed a flow control ordinance in a case that involved deciding whether two New York counties may direct locally collected trash to a publicly owned transfer and separation facility. In *United Haulers Association v. Oneida-Herkimer Solid Waste Management Authority* the Court ruled that Oneida and Herkimer Counties could direct trash to their publicly owned facility without violating the dormant Commerce Clause. The majority's opinion held that the local government ordinance was aimed at a number of legitimate goals, such as ensuring proper handling of waste, unrelated to economic protectionism: "The flow control ordinances in this case benefit a clearly public facility, while treating all private companies exactly the same. . . . We hold that the Counties' flow control ordinances, which treat in-state private businesses exactly the same as out-of-state ones, do not 'discriminate against interstate commerce' for the purposes of the dormant Commerce Clause."[15]

The Court also recognized that the ordinances achieve important public goals by allowing residents to recycle and deposit hazardous waste for free. Interestingly, among those filing *amici curiae* briefs in this case were two Virginia counties, Sussex and Charles City, which host mega-landfills within their borders. Those Virginia counties opposed the New York ordinances on the grounds that they diminish the flow of waste across state lines, thereby interfering with interstate commerce.[16]

Court challenges to local constraints on the flow of trash have been seen elsewhere around the country. In 2006 the City of Red Wing, Minnesota, enacted an ordinance that would force local haulers to take trash to the local incinerator, which faces declining revenues because its tipping fees are higher than those in surrounding areas. A federal district court granted a preliminary injunction against the ordinance on the grounds that it discriminates against interstate commerce by preventing local haulers from taking trash. A Daviess County, Kentucky, ordinance that would award waste collection franchises only to haulers who use the county's disposal facilities was overturned in both federal district and appeals courts. Following the Supreme Court's affirmation of the Oneida-Herkimer ordinances, the Court granted certiorari for the Daviess County case and vacated the Sixth Circuit's decision.[17]

In an unusual case involving the flow of garbage across international borders, Michigan residents and politicians have objected to the flow of garbage from Toronto, Ontario. In 2006 the Michigan legislature passed, and Governor Jennifer Granholm signed, a bill that would abrogate contracts between landfills and non-state entities should Congress give states the right to ban Canadian garbage. Michigan's senators and representatives introduced congressional legislation that would grant states that right. In response, the City of Toronto agreed to reduce the amount of waste sent to Michigan by 20 percent in 2007 and by 40 percent in 2008, with a complete phase-out by 2010. Toronto aims to achieve this goal in large part through recycling and source reduction, which are already at relatively high levels. In 2005 Toronto estimated that 40 percent of the City's trash was diverted into recycling or source reduction.[18]

State and local attempts to control the flow of municipal solid waste arise from contradictory impulses. For the most part, local governments who enact trash transport constraints want to keep trash within their borders. By contrast, state governments tend to object to the "trashing" of land and waterways within their borders and thus many state governments want to restrict the flow of garbage into their jurisdictions. These contradictions have resulted in garbage wars that pit states against other states, counties against counties, and states against their own counties and cities. Importing state governments have proposed laws that would block entirely or tax differentially waste coming from out of state, in the name of preserving landfill capacity or ensuring that there are sufficient funds to pay for associated pollution problems. Exporting states have challenged those efforts as violating the dormant Commerce Clause.

Some local governments have attempted to funnel locally generated waste to locally supported facilities. Other local governments have become dependent on the revenue streams generated by mega-landfills, which import trash from faraway cities and towns. Those areas object to flow control enacted by other counties, since that might reduce the amount of trash sent to their facilities, and they also oppose any state-imposed constraint on the flow of trash across state lines.[19]

These battles over who should control the flow of garbage have spilled into the Congress. In the following section I describe those efforts, the goals they aim to achieve, and the reactions they have provoked. As of this writing, none of these bills has been enacted, and most bills never reached a committee or subcommittee vote. But their sponsors persist in introducing them, an indication that some constituencies feel intensely about these issues.

CONGRESSIONAL BILLS TO ALLOW CONSTRAINTS ON THE FLOW OF TRASH

The first general thing of note about legislative efforts to limit the flow of trash is the sheer number of bills that have been crafted. Between the 101st (1989–90) and the 110th (2007–8) Congresses there were 159 such bills, House and Senate combined, with the largest proportion of these introduced in the early 1990s.[20] Proposed bills in Congress that have targeted interstate waste transport have had two main thrusts: first, to allow local areas to control the outgoing flow of locally generated municipal solid waste; and second, to allow states to erect various kinds of restrictions on the incoming flow of municipal solid waste generated elsewhere. Democrats and Republicans alike have introduced these pieces of legislation. As is often the case with the Congress, perceived constituent interests have trumped partisan affiliation. Not surprisingly, the primary architects of trash flow legislation have been senators and representatives from importing states like Pennsylvania, Virginia, Michigan, and Ohio. None of these proposed bills was enacted into law. Most bills were duly referred to the appropriate committees or subcommittees and did not see the legislative light of day thereafter.

Several bills aimed to authorize localities to control the flow of locally generated trash. One representative bill that was introduced in 1999 by Senator Arlen Specter of Pennsylvania would have permitted flow controls by localities over local waste under certain conditions. Senator Specter's proposal had three important elements. First, only facilities that had flow control in place prior to the 1994 *Carbone v. Clarkstown* decision would have been allowed to reinstate their ordinances. Second, the waste to be controlled would need to be generated within the state or local jurisdiction. Finally, government authorities would have been required to demonstrate financial or contractual dependence on the waste whose flow was to be controlled once again. Legislation proposed by Senator Voinovich (Ohio) had many features in common with that of Senator Specter. Other flow control proposals were more open-ended. For example, Representative David Minge of Minnesota introduced a bill that would have allowed any government authority to establish local flow control, with no strings attached.[21]

Advocates of reinstating local flow control have argued two points— one financial, one environmental. The financial concern goes to the use of flow control to ensure reliable funding for waste management facilities. Many such facilities were financed prior to the 1994 *Carbone* decision under the assumption of guaranteed waste flows that would bring in predictable streams of revenue. Flow control supporters also claim that its reinstatement would help local governments ensure that waste is handled in an environmentally protective manner and that recycling and waste-reduction goals are met. Keeping trash at home allows local authorities to use trash revenues to support recycling and source reduction, goals that might not be met if garbage is sent to other waste management facilities.

In what was perhaps the broadest effort to institutionalize local flow control, the New Jersey state legislature required in 1978 that every county develop a waste management plan. The state also enacted flow control legislation. These actions followed the perception of a waste disposal crisis characterized by dwindling in-state disposal capacity and escalating out-of-state disposal costs. In his testimony before the Senate Environment and Public Works Committee, following the *Carbone* decision, Representative Bob Franks spoke of widespread fears that local governments would default on the $1.7 billion worth of bonds that had been issued to construct these facilities. Since that time the state has helped counties make debt payments and has forgiven some state loans, but the state's most recent Solid Waste Management Plan claims that "Once financially secure disposal facilities are struggling to maintain systems burdened with significant 'stranded' debt since the Carbone and Atlantic Coast federal court decisions."[22]

Other waste management districts faced financial problems as a result of the *Carbone* decision. In his 1997 testimony before the Senate Environment and Public Works Committee, Randy Johnson, then head of the Hennepin, Minnesota, County Board of Commissioners, cited approximately thirty examples of counties or solid waste authorities across the country who had lost substantial amounts of revenue and/or whose bond ratings had been downgraded as a result of the *Carbone* decision. At that same hearing a host of counties wrote in support of legislation sanctioning flow control. John Skinner, the president of the Solid Waste Association of North America (SWANA), which at the time represented 6,400 local government and private solid waste professionals, advocated reinstating flow control for local governments left with stranded debt.[23]

Although SWANA has stopped lobbying actively for flow control, the National Association of Counties (NACo) still claims that the *Carbone* decision "caused countless problems for many counties across the United States, especially those that made pre-Carbone financial commitments based on reliance on flow control authority. The consequences of Carbone have been scores of lawsuits and prolonged litigation for many flow control–reliant local governments, bond downgrades, curtailed capital expenditures for waste management and other services, termination of recycling and other vital environmental programs, increased local taxes and user fees, and default on bond indenture requirements."[24]

NACo supports congressional attempts to authorize the use of flow control by localities over the trash generated within their borders. In NACo's view, flow control appropriately keeps trash at home and it guarantees local governments revenue that can be used to design environmentally protective facilities, thereby providing a shield against possible future liability claims that might result from dumping trash at less-protective waste management facilities. The fear of future liability claims has its roots in the fact that many current Superfund sites were once landfills.

In defending its local monopoly over waste management before the Supreme Court, the Oneida-Herkimer Solid Waste Management Authority echoed these concerns and supplemented its theoretical claims with vivid local examples. The Authority provided one of the most compelling cases on record for why some flow control, even if it is somewhat more costly in the short term, is preferred by some local governments. The counties' detailed history of the environmental and financial burdens imposed by private landfills is worth quoting at length:

> A 1969 planning study conducted for Oneida and Herkimer Counties identified 44 operating dump sites, both public and private, all of which posed varying degrees of threat to public health and the environment. In the early 1980's, health officials ordered the closure of drinking water wells near several of these facilities. Twelve of these sites were ultimately identified as inactive hazardous waste disposal sites by State and Federal authorities. One, the privately operated Ludlow landfill in the Town of Paris, Oneida County, was named to the National Priorities List (Superfund) pursuant to the Comprehensive Environmental Response, Compensation, and Liability Act of 1980. . . .
>
> Clean-up and remediation costs at these sites totaled over $74 million. In the case of the Ludlow landfill, regulatory action by the state to compel its closure led to wider litigation, in which over 600 local businesses, municipalities (29 of them) and other generators, were named as third-party defendants in a cost recovery action. Of the 44 operating dump sites in 1969, only one was operating at the time these local laws were adopted in early 1990.
>
> The private sector provided no solutions. In 1986, only the privately-operated Mohawk Valley landfill was available to serve the

City of Utica, and its operators doubled their fees to the City on short notice. Mohawk Valley was itself unlined, operating without a state permit, and under regulatory pressure to close. In September 1986, local haulers, including two of the plaintiffs in this case, called upon the Counties to develop a new regional landfill as a safeguard against the closure of Mohawk Valley, which finally occurred in 1992.[25]

However, flow control is strenuously opposed by waste management companies, by private haulers, and by other local governments that have become dependent on the revenues generated by accepting garbage from far-away locations. Their rationales are fairly straightforward: like other items of commerce, trash should be allowed to flow to waste management facilities near or far, as the market dictates. This will ensure that MSW generators or local government authorities can select the cheapest, most appropriate waste disposal services. Enhanced competition will ensure that waste management facilities offer services cost-effectively. Wherever the waste goes, it will be handled in a safe, environmentally protective manner because of state and federal regulations for modern landfills and incinerators.

In his comments at hearings concerning a 2002 bill introduced by Senator Specter, Senator Bob Smith (New Hampshire) summed up many of these sentiments:

> The need for flow control implies the inability to compete in a free market system—which means residents would be paying prices higher than they would otherwise be paying. It is, in essence, an added tax on top of paying for waste management services for anyone who lives within these jurisdictions. But when forced to compete, the majority of communities have risen to the occasion by charging competitive rates, streamlining operational costs and seeking alternative sources of revenues. I commend these communities for responding with innovation and good old American ingenuity. Now, if localities need to raise additional revenue, they can do so without compromising the free market mechanism. If localities want to impose a tax on their citizens, they should do so directly, rather than hiding it in Federal flow control legislation.[26]

No flow control legislation has been introduced in the Congress since 2003.[27]

BILLS TO ERECT INTERSTATE BARRIERS TO THE FLOW OF TRASH

The second category of proposed bills in Congress would allow states to erect various kinds of restrictions on the incoming flow of municipal solid waste generated elsewhere. Such bills have tended to share the common feature that states would be allowed to constrain the movement of trash from other states. Other characteristics have varied among these proposed bills, including the number of states that could enact waste transport restrictions, the conditions under which local governments could win exemptions to those restrictions, and the presence or absence of differentiated garbage taxes. As with proposed bills authorizing local flow control, none of these proposed bills has been enacted into law.

One such piece of legislation, focusing on international shipments of waste, was passed in the House of Representatives in 2006 and was referred to the Senate Committee on Environment and Public Works. Had it been enacted, the International Solid Waste Importation and Management Act of 2006 would have allowed states to restrict the "receipt or disposal" of municipal solid waste from other countries until the Administrator of the Environmental Protection Agency issued regulations implementing and enforcing the Agreement Concerning the Transboundary Movement of Hazardous Waste between the United States and Canada.[28] That Agreement provides only for notification of waste flowing between Canada and the United States and does not constrain trash movement in any way. The intent of this proposed legislation appears to have been to implement a more draconian solution, allowing states to restrict waste from Canada, until the more mild Agreement was implemented properly in the U.S. Since Toronto has since agreed to phase out export of trash to Michigan by 2010, it seems unlikely that Congress will enact this legislation.

Other proposed bills have focused on blocking interstate transport of waste. For example, the late Representative Jo Ann Davis of Williamsburg, Virginia, introduced in the 110th Congress the same two bills she had sponsored previously. One of these proposals would have allowed states to restrict the import of trash through a variety of measures, including: one tax rate for in-state trash and another for out-of-state trash; limits on the percentage of out-of-state trash received at specific landfills or incinerators; and freezing out-of-state levels. Under this proposal, states could not interfere with existing host community agreements until two years after the bill's enactment. Davis's other proposal would have enacted a presumptive ban on the acceptance of out-of-state garbage at landfills or incinerators, unless that waste management facility had entered into a host community agreement. This bill would also have allowed states to limit the amount of out-of-state waste received at in-state landfills and incinerators.[29]

On the Senate side, Ohio Senator Voinovich, with co-sponsors from Indiana, Ohio, Michigan, Wisconsin, Oregon, and Virginia, introduced bills in the 106th and 107th Congresses that would have prohibited facilities from receiving out-of-state waste for disposal unless the waste were received pursuant to a new or existing host community agreement or other State authorization. This legislation would also have allowed states to cap the amount of waste received from other states, as long as the exporting states were notified of those limits, and it would have permitted "cost recovery surcharges" on out-of-state waste of up to $3/ton. Those funds were to be used for solid waste management programs.[30]

Attempts to constrain MSW movement across state lines have often been bipartisan. In 1999 Virginia Senators John Warner and Charles Robb jointly sponsored a bill that would have allowed a handful of the highest-importing states to restrict interstate waste transport, even to the point of banning waste from "super exporting" states. This bill would have allowed local governments to request a waiver for their landfill or, alternatively, they could be exempted on the basis of an existing host community agreement.[31]

Opponents of bills blocking transport of waste over state lines argue that such measures are ill considered environmentally and economically. In their view, it makes little sense to force states like Rhode Island or New Jersey, for example, with high population density and little available land, to bury their own trash or incinerator ash. According to these arguments, Virginia's clay soils form a better line of defense against groundwater contamination than more permeable soils. The state's waterways and interstate highways, combined with an abundance of sparsely populated areas, are among the geographically specific factors that make it an arguably better location for landfills than more densely populated states. Another assertion is that trash generators (including households) will inevitably pay more to dispose of trash that is not allowed to flow "with the market."

Finally, one might question the implicit claim that trash from out of state is more harmful to Virginia's rural landfills than is trash coming from other parts of the state. There is no immediately obvious reason for why trash flowing to southeastern Virginia's mega-landfills from more urbanized areas in central and northern Virginia should be treated more generously than trash flowing from urban areas in other states or from the District of Columbia. In this line of reasoning, all that matters is that trash flowing into mega-landfills does so with the informed consent of the surrounding community. The trash's ultimate geographic source is irrelevant.

Moreover, officials from exporting areas like the City New York resist being labeled as environmentally irresponsible. They point out that MSW formerly dumped at environmentally disastrous facilities like the Fresh Kills Landfill is now moving to much more modern, secure sites. City officials also claim that they will contract only with companies that have signed host community agreements with the local authorities that signify local consent and that provide compensation in the form of per-ton fees and taxes. Bruce Parker, president of the National Solid Wastes Management Association, has claimed that "Many communities view waste disposal as just another type of economic activity. . . . These communities agree to host landfills and in exchange receive benefits, which are often called host community fees, that help build schools, buy fire trucks and police cars, and hire teachers, firemen and policemen and keep the local tax base lower."[32]

In congressional and judicial discussions over the flow of trash we see reflected the fundamental debate identified at the start of this book. If MSW is primarily a health and environmental threat, state and local governments argue that they should be able to constrain its movement to protect current and future generations from its pernicious effects and to minimize the associated financial burdens. If MSW is primarily an article of commerce with benefits accruing to trash generators, landfill owners, and host communities, then it is argued that we should promote its free, unrestricted trade.

TRASH, POLLUTION, COMMERCE, AND PUBLIC EDUCATION FUNDING

The debates over whether trash is primarily pollution or commerce illuminate conflicting interests among state and local government authorities. Local governments are responsible for ensuring trash removal and thus, even when local governments turn trash collection over to private haulers, trash looms as a responsibility and, therefore, a cost. Local government authorities need more revenue to support waste management programs than was previously the case, because of the costs associated with environmentally protective disposal and recycling.

As a consequence, many municipalities, from New York City to Charlottesville, Virginia, have chosen to ship their waste elsewhere, often to privately run transfer stations, incinerators, or landfills. The fees received by landfill host communities not only underwrite construction and maintenance costs for waste management facilities, they support local services like schools and police departments.

When local taxes must be relied on for school funding, it is easy to understand the attraction of "trash-for-cash" arrangements. States differ considerably in the extent to which local vs. state government funding is used to pay for schools. The National Education Association regularly reports the relative proportion of education funding provided by state vs. local governments. Of the eleven states with the highest trash imports in 2005, only four provided more than the U.S. median revenue from the state level, while seven provided less than the median level. In 2005–6 Virginia state government provided 39.6 percent of K–12 public school revenues and local governments provided 57.3 percent, while the national medians for these statistics were 46.8 and 49.0 percent, respectively. In Pennsylvania, which still imports the highest amount of MSW in the U.S., the state provided only 35.4 percent of revenue for public schools, as contrasted with 62.5 percent provided by local government. In the face of these figures, it is hard to escape the conclusion that relatively low state funding for schools has increased the incentives for local governments to look elsewhere, even at trash, for steady revenue streams.[33]

In contrast with local governments, state governments regard trash as an unmitigated environmental liability with no economically redeeming qualities. State government officials point to the certainty that all landfills, even modern ones, will eventually leak. Many former landfills have become federal or state Superfund sites whose cleanup has run into the millions of dollars. For example, the Kim-Stan Landfill in Selma, Virginia, which lies in the west-central portion of the state, accepted much of its waste from out of state. The environmental contamination caused by this Superfund site has cost Virginia millions of dollars for cleanup and EPA estimates that the federal government will spend $8 million in remedial action costs.[34]

In Senate testimony, the director of the Virginia Department of Environmental Quality, Robert Burnley, described the connections between the state's view on accepting out-of-state waste, on the one hand, and, on the other hand, the burdens imposed by the Kim-Stan landfill:

The U.S. EPA acknowledges that despite our best technology, *all landfills will leak eventually.* Virginia has enacted very stringent requirements for the siting, monitoring and operation of its landfills, more stringent than those established by EPA. Despite our best efforts to protect Virginia's environment, however, we do not know what will happen twenty or thirty years from now. Common sense tells us that the larger the landfill and the more waste we are forced to accept, the greater the risks of ground water contamination and other pollution.

Unfortunately, Virginia has already suffered the consequences of uncontrolled shipment of out-of-state waste. The Kim-Stan Landfill in western Virginia was originally operated as a local landfill but was later purchased by private interests. In the subsequent months they began importing waste from other states, increasing the volume significantly. Hundreds of tractor-trailers filled with trash traveled the back roads of rural Allegheny County each day. The owners soon filed bankruptcy and the landfill is now a Superfund site. The Commonwealth has already expended millions of its taxpayer dollars to investigate and contain the contamination; neither the generators nor the generating state have borne any of these costs. We hope our enhanced landfill regulations will prevent this type of environmental catastrophe from happening in the future, but the fact remains that no one is certain that current landfill designs are adequate to provide long-term environmental protection.[35]

Although EPA reimburses Virginia for some of the costs incurred in Superfund site cleanup, a 1995 report completed for the Virginia General Assembly estimated that cleanup of contaminated waste sites would require between $277 million and $670 million in total. In the Commonwealth's biennial 2004–6 budget the Virginia General Assembly allocated only $7 million for waste disposal site remediation.[36]

States faced with environmental cleanup costs cannot collect from responsible out-of-state generators. Thus, many state governments regard trash as an environmental time bomb, at least some of whose cleanup costs are imposed from out of state but will be borne by state taxpayers alone. Lacking permission from Congress, state governments cannot now assess differential fees on out-of-state trash to help underwrite the costs of future contamination problems. However, it is possible, as Pennsylvania has done, to assess uniform fees on all trash deposited at in-state landfills and to deposit those funds in a special state cleanup fund.

In the environmental arena state governments are often aided by federal funds. The Environmental Protection Agency helps pay for the cleanup of Superfund sites like the Kim-Stan Landfill. Superfund monies formerly came largely from industry taxes, under the "polluter pays" principle. But since that taxing authority expired in 1995 the general public has assumed an increasing share of Superfund's costs, to the point that 60 percent of Superfund's resources now come from general government revenue whose source, of course, is federal taxpayers.[37] Whether Superfund's costs are spread among the petrochemical industry or more broadly among the American public, one might argue that, at least for the fraction of contaminated landfills that are designated Superfund sites, some small part of the cleanup costs is borne by residents of exporting municipalities who contributed trash to other states. Still, state governments justifiably fear the future liabilities associated with leaks from MSW landfills.

The irony is that some of the top importing states have indirectly helped to foster the flow of trash across their borders. Schools are the lifeblood of any community. As pointed out above, Virginia and Pennsylvania are among the states that distribute relatively low percentages of state funding for schools. This creates a revenue vacuum that can be filled through local property taxes in affluent, densely populated communities. But less-wealthy rural communities have looked to fees from private waste management firms to fund their schools and other public services. In rural Virginia and elsewhere, local government authorities have seemingly decided that landfill revenue is preferable to inadequate revenue.

Perhaps one of the policy problems to be solved in this arena has nothing to do with long-distance trash transport per se and everything to do with the relative generosity or stinginess of states with respect to school funding. This way of framing the problem is completely absent from national deliberations about flow control and interstate waste transport.

In the final chapter, I summarize the problems that have emerged in this analysis and I connect those problems with the appropriate policy solutions.

CHAPTER 5

Solving the Genuine Problems of Long-Distance Trash Transport

In the classic expression of the policymaking process, problems are identified and then the appropriate solutions are formulated. But, to adapt a well-known expression to the policymaking world, many's the slip between problem identification and policy solution. Sometimes the problems are incorrectly or imprecisely described. At other times the problems are properly identified, but the solutions proposed are either unwieldy or wrong-headed or, alternatively, they would cause unwanted or unintended consequences.

In this final chapter I conclude that proposed legislation permitting states to constrain the interstate flow of trash into their jurisdictions fails to address the primary policy problems at hand, which are:

- Americans make too much garbage.
- Long-distance transport likely creates more air and water pollution relative to disposing of trash closer to its point of origin.
- Mega-landfills concentrate huge amounts of trash and, despite the fact that they must install modern environmental protections, they will inevitably create future contamination problems.

- Landfills are often located in economically and politically vulnerable areas whose residents have few resources and little power to mount opposition or to consider alternatives.

First I explain why interstate trash transport is not the policy problem to be solved and how adopting the kinds of solutions proposed in Congress could well create perverse, unintended consequences. Then I suggest two sets of proposed policy solutions to the more-genuine problems articulated above.

The first set of solutions recommends an expanded role for the national government in MSW diversion, reduction, and regulation. The United States Environmental Protection Agency should:

- set national waste diversion goals;
- more actively promote pay-as-you-throw programs;
- regulate the disposal of electronic product and household hazardous waste; and
- study the possibility of instituting extended producer responsibility programs for common types of non-hazardous waste, like packaging.

The second set of solutions aims to protect future generations and today's socioeconomically vulnerable communities from bearing unfair environmental burdens. Specifically, I recommend that the federal government:

- assess a new national tax on garbage to pay for current and future environmental contamination at waste disposal sites and to create disincentives for MSW production;
- establish through the RCRA solid waste planning process new procedural safeguards for communities that have accepted, or that might accept, new waste disposal facilities;
- write federal guidelines on compensation for landfill or incinerator host communities; and
- adopt some version of the proximity principle, using a modified, U.S.-appropriate version of the policies that have been established in the European Union and Japan.

Despite the fact that the proximity principle has been embraced in the European Union and in Japan, its relevance here is not immediately obvious, since Americans on the whole are not as space-constrained as are the Europeans and Japanese. However, the proximity principle's normative underpinnings are compelling, irrespective of the fact that, relatively speaking, Americans still have ample dumping grounds. Flow control ordinances represent a version of the proximity principle in that they express the desire of local governments to oversee the environmental management of waste generated in their communities. But to date flow control has been implemented only at the local level. I advocate here exploring the possibility of applying the proximity principle more widely in the U.S., using the EU's approach as a starting point.

WHY INTERSTATE TRASH TRANSPORT PER SE IS NOT THE PROBLEM

Members of Congress and state government officials have raised four fundamental objections to interstate trash transport. First, states claim that in-state disposal capacity is consumed too quickly and that state and local governments "lose control" of their landfill capacity when thousands of tons are imported from neighboring states. Second, state officials assert that it is difficult to screen out-of-state waste for possible hazardous or infectious waste and that the cost of resulting contamination problems will fall on state taxpayers as there is no legal recourse to collect funds from out-of-state municipalities, businesses, or individuals. Third, they object to pollution and safety problems associated with truck, train, or barge transport. Finally, state officials from importing states claim that those exporting trash have no incentive to develop "responsible" waste management schemes that, for example, stress recycling and source reduction, because they can simply transport their garbage elsewhere.

To illustrate this last claim, in 2002 David Hess, then Secretary of Pennsylvania's Department of Environmental Protection, pointed to his state's concerted recycling and materials reuse programs and contrasted them with New York City's decision to suspend temporarily recycling for metals, glass, and plastics for eighteen months. Hess complained that the City of New York had decided in essence to dump its trash on other jurisdictions rather than reduce the waste stream through recycling. The

City has struggled over the years to find sufficient processing capacity for its huge volume of recyclables and the 9/11 crisis diverted the City's attention to more pressing matters. However, the City has recently strengthened its recycling program and a recent report estimates its recycling rate at 30.6 percent. The City's Solid Waste Management Plan wants to achieve an overall MSW diversion rate of 70 percent by 2015. The City's Budget Office projects that a vigorous recycling program will not only divert MSW from landfills, it will be less costly on a per-ton basis than exporting trash, because the per-ton costs of collection decrease with volume.[1]

These efforts notwithstanding, the concerns expressed by Secretary Hess are legitimate. It makes sense that waste generators should pay to take care of the pollution created by their waste. It is possible that some municipalities can more cheaply send their waste to landfills than to recycling facilities, thereby creating a disincentive for strong recycling programs. The specter of a landscape pocked with landfills is understandably unwelcome in any state.

But these problems are not created solely—or even primarily—by out-of-state MSW generators. After all, many cities within Virginia have elected to shut down their local landfills and send their waste to central and southeastern Virginia's regional waste disposal facilities. Sixty-five percent of MSW disposed in Virginia's landfills originates in Virginia, and each ton of trash, no matter whether generated two hundred miles away within-state or out-of-state, has the same potential to contaminate the environment at any given landfill. No document that I have seen has established that New York City's MSW is more toxic than that generated in Virginia.[2]

Furthermore, the directional flow of trash across state borders shifts over time, and many neighboring states, especially those with large urban areas at shared borders, have long traded in MSW. Philadelphia's garbage once flowed into New Jersey and now some of New Jersey's trash flows into Pennsylvania. MSW exported to Virginia from the District of Columbia crosses state lines, but it's difficult to argue that the District's trash is somehow worse for central and southeastern Virginia landfills than trash transported from the northern Virginia suburbs just across the Potomac River from the District.

In other words, asking whether the MSW crossed state lines seems less important environmentally than asking, how far did the MSW travel from point of generation to point of disposal? Long-distance trash transport, whether by rail, truck, or barge, can be harmful because of associated air and water pollution. Trash leaking from barges clearly has the potential to cause harm to waterways in Virginia and elsewhere. By one estimate, trash truck traffic around New York City after the Fresh Kills Landfill closed increased by 256,000 trips per year, which at the time amounted to 2 percent of all traffic through bridges and tunnels to New Jersey. In 1998 a truck moving trash from New York to Virginia crashed on the beltway around Washington, D.C., killing two and injuring seven. During one trash truck "sting" Pennsylvania police took 34 percent of trucks off of the road because their violations were so serious. In 1999 eight northeastern states (including Virginia and Pennsylvania) conducted a three-day crackdown on trash trucks and issued more than four thousand violations.[3]

These statistics regarding the hazards of long-distance truck transport are alarming. But allowing some states to erect barriers to trash is likely to simply deflect trash to other areas, and thus state-imposed barriers to trash are not likely to solve the problem of transport-related pollution. There are more-effective, more-direct methods of controlling transport-related pollution. For example, the State of Wisconsin has received an EPA grant to reduce diesel emissions from trash trucks. Barge transporters of solid waste in Virginia must meet the Commonwealth's Waste Management Board's regulations that require verifiably watertight containers and that limit the height to which containers may be stacked. Pennsylvania has adopted standards for vehicles carrying MSW to facilities within that state. Enforcement actions against trash trucks can catch unsafe vehicles and serve as a warning to others to keep their trucks in good order. Part of the solution to the problem of transport-related pollution lies in strict national or state vehicle emissions and safety standards that are enforced effectively. If fuel costs rise again, the resulting increase in transportation costs may well discourage long-distance MSW movement.[4]

Allowing states to cap or freeze the amount of trash imported from other states might also have adverse consequences for local governments, many of whom have accepted mega-landfills in exchange for host fees that underwrite needed local services. If part of the policy problem is that state governments sometimes do not provide an adequate share of funding for schools and other local services, then it seems perverse to allow states to enact limits on trash transport that would only perpetuate that imbalance by denying needed local revenue. However, helping local governments prevent and remediate contamination from these massive landfills is vital, and that issue is addressed later in this chapter. Further, given the concentration of mega-landfills in central and southeastern Virginia, the state should establish a statewide strategic planning process for MSW facilities.

Finally, enforcing some of the proposed constraints on the interstate flow of trash could be difficult and administratively burdensome. For example, it is unclear how a state would implement a "freeze" on imported trash at levels realized in a prior year. Would the frozen trash allowances be divided up among solid-waste generators within the exporting state? It seems likely that voluminous recordkeeping and heavy administrative oversight would be necessary to ensure that landfills and incinerators complied with such restrictions. Arguably, enforcement resources would be better spent in ensuring the environmental integrity of those sites.

Several legitimate policy problems have emerged from the debate over trash transport. States have reason to worry about how they will pay for environmental contamination from waste sites now and in the future. Preserving overall landfill capacity is a desirable goal, as our population and waste generation per capita continue to grow. While the United States currently has an ample supply of potential landfill space, that resource should not be squandered. Once land is used for landfilling, many other productive uses of that land are foreclosed forever, even after the landfill is closed. We should also take care to mitigate the pollution associated with transporting trash over long distances.

However, constraining the cross-border flow of trash is an indirect and convoluted method of addressing these issues. It also handicaps local governments that are trying to take care of their communities when funds from the state government or from local property taxes are in short supply. These problems can and should be addressed in other ways.

POLICY SOLUTION I: WASTE DIVERSION AND REDUCTION

The analysis presented in chapter 2 shows that each American makes at least one-third more—and perhaps more than twice as much—trash as his or her European Union or Japanese counterpart. By comparison with other industrialized nations, MSW production in the U.S. per unit of economic productivity might be average or it could exceed median industrialized nation rates by two-thirds. Americans' apparent wastefulness is counterbalanced by increasing recycling rates, which, despite more intensive efforts, still lag behind those in the European Union and in Japan.

Aggressive efforts to reduce and divert waste in European Union Member States and in Japan ripple through the waste management system and are reflected in relatively high disposal costs. Disposing of waste by landfilling is discouraged in the EU and in Japan, and national regulatory pressures have been brought to bear on waste production. For example, the European Union's landfill directive instructs Member States to reduce biodegradable waste (which includes paper) sent to landfills by 65 percent in 2020 relative to 1995 levels. To give one concrete example of what this means: in the United Kingdom biodegradable waste constitutes 60 percent of the waste stream, which means that by 2020 MSW sent to landfills must be reduced by 39 percent overall.

In both Japan and the European Union governments and citizens have embraced pollution prevention for its own sake to a greater extent than is the case in the United States. In the European Union, packaging waste, electronic products, and biodegradable waste have all been subjected to aggressive pollution prevention measures, including education, taxes, and waste segregation requirements. In some cases these measures have saved money through avoided waste disposal.[5]

In contrast with these efforts, national government authorities in the United States have made only symbolic gestures in the direction of reducing the amount of trash we produce or to diverting waste from landfills to more productive uses like composting. The U.S. Environmental Protection Agency offers a per capita daily goal of 4.3 lbs/capita of MSW, as compared with current levels of 4.6 lbs/capita, and a 35 percent recycling rate goal, as compared with the current national rate of 33 percent.[6] No regulatory programs are associated with achieving these modest goals because Congress has not given EPA regulatory authority for reducing MSW generation or for enforcing recycling rates.

State and municipal governments have tried to increase recycling rates and to reduce the amount of waste sent to landfills. The techniques employed to achieve these ends have included mandates. Seattle, Washington mandates recycling for certain materials. Residents or businesses who are found to have greater than 10 percent of those items in their trash risk losing their trash collection until they recycle properly. Businesses can be fined for throwing away recyclables.[7] Other programs employ incentive-based schemes.

These programs attempt to overcome the erroneous perception among American citizens and businesses that throwing stuff away has no cost. Historical evidence indicates that when urban trash collection was first instituted in the early twentieth century, people began to toss out household items that previously they would have reused.[8] In many cities members of the public have until recently viewed trash collection and disposal as "free" because their costs were hidden in property taxes. There is no incentive to reduce waste because property taxes do not vary with the amount of trash one produces. Homeowners paying identical property taxes but generating vastly different amounts of trash effectively pay the same rate for MSW services. In such schemes, recycling rates tend to be lower than they are in pay-as-you-throw schemes that charge according to the amount of discarded waste but that allow for free recycling.

An example of an MSW management program that does not create incentives for recycling or reduced trash production can be found in the District of Columbia. Here, the city government does not charge for trash collection as a function of the amount generated. Large recycling bins are provided and residents are encouraged to use them for a wide range of recyclable items. Despite the easy availability of curbside recycling, the District's residential trash diversion rate was only 17 percent in 2007. And the combined commercial and residential recycling rate was a dismal 18 percent in 2007. Both rates fall far short of the District's official recycling goal of 45 percent and the national rate of 33 percent. Of course, diversion rates can also vary as a function of public education and program funding, and it seems likely that more intensive campaigns, supported by a stronger budget, might help increase the District's low diversion rate. The District's recycling office employs only nine people.[9]

Pay-as-you-throw fees, which vary according to the amount of trash disposed, make waste management costs visible to waste generators, they encourage recycling, and they have the potential to reduce the amount of waste produced. One study by the Solid Waste Management Association of North American indicates that variable-rate pricing for trash collection increases recycling rates on average by 5 to 6 percent. In one New Hampshire town the introduction of pay-as-you-throw trash collection increased recycling rates from 2 percent to 30 percent in less than a year and decreased the amount of trash sent to landfills by 60 percent.[10] Variable-rate pricing is fundamentally fair in that citizens generating small amounts of trash do not subsidize those generating more trash. Rather, as with electricity or gas, one pays for the amount of service used. Trash fee subsidies can and should be provided to low-income families.

Pay-as-you-throw programs have been adopted in an estimated 6,000 cities and towns. For example, such programs can be found in 110 of Massachusetts's 351 towns and cities. The City of San Francisco aims to divert 100 percent of its MSW from landfills by 2020, and pay-as-you-throw programs are among the tools employed to reach this ambitious target. In 2006 San Franciscans diverted two-thirds of their waste streams from landfills. San Francisco is using other innovative tools to meet these ambitious goals. For example, the City has started to collect pet manure and transform it into methane, which can then be used as a fuel.[11]

Despite the growing popularity of pay-as-you-throw programs, some communities find hurdles to its public acceptance. In one Connecticut town one citizen reacted to the prospect of paying directly for trash by bombing a trailer filled with the city's supply of new trash bags. When cities and towns implement pay-as-you-throw programs without reducing property taxes in parallel, some citizens may resist the imposition of what seems to be a new tax. However, waste management costs can rise over time, and paying for some portion of those costs through pay-as-you-throw programs is fairer than paying through property taxes. Many such programs cover all or a large portion of a municipality's waste management costs. Some observers claim that roadside dumping increases when pay-as-you-throw programs are instituted, but few studies are available to support this claim. One longtime solid waste superintendent in Mansfield, Connecticut, contends, "I've been in this business on both coasts taking care of garbage for almost thirty years, and whenever we propose anything new with garbage, opponents say there will be more garbage on the side of the road. . . . But there's always garbage on the side of the road."[12]

Some businesses have championed the waste reduction cause, thereby reinforcing government-based efforts. Wal-Mart has announced that, like the City of San Francisco, the company wishes to "create zero waste," and its goal for 2008 was to reduce the company's MSW by 25 percent. Xerox aims to produce "waste free products in waste free facilities," and claims that in 2004 the company diverted more than a hundred million pounds (50,000 tons) of waste through recycling and reuse. Xerox achieves extraordinary recycling rates: 83 percent (or 29,000 Mg) of process manufacturing waste (which includes paper, pallets, packaging, batteries, etc.) was recycled in 2005, and 98 percent (or 37,000 Mg) of "equipment waste" (returned products) was reused. Since 1991 Fetzer Vineyards has reduced by 93 percent the amount of its waste sent to landfills. Computer products manufacturer Epson Portland Inc. has sent no waste to landfills since 2000, and the company has reduced its overall amount of waste by 95 percent since 1999. Several thermostat manufacturers have established the Thermostat Recycling Corporation, which organizes the collection and return to manufacturers of mercury-containing thermostats. Such companies not only seek ways of reducing the amount of waste produced, they voluntarily assume responsibility for the waste streams associated with their products.[13]

By contrast, "extended producer responsibility" programs force companies through government fiat to take back various forms of waste, thereby "extending" their "responsibility" for the waste generated by their products through the product's post-consumer stage. The idea is to shift the burden for product waste to manufacturers so they will internalize the environmental costs of their products and have an incentive to consider waste reduction as they design their products. No such programs exist at the national level in the United States, but some states have enacted such programs for selected products.

Perhaps the oldest and most widely established form of extended producer responsibility is found with beverage container deposit programs, which exist in eleven states. New York State requires that all cell phone companies take back up to ten phones per household and that the companies provide free shipping for phone return. California prohibits many electronic devices from being sent to waste disposal facilities and charges consumers an advance recycling fee of several dollars that is refunded to manufacturers or electronics recyclers to pay for recycling programs. Maine also has a mandatory take-back program for electronic devices.[14]

Canadian provinces and the European Union have been more aggressive in instituting extended producer responsibility programs. For example, Alberta has instituted advance recycling fees for beverage containers, tires, used oil, oil containers, oil filters, and electronics. British Columbia's extended producer responsibility program started in the early 1970s with the first bottle deposit program in North America. Now the province's comprehensive program includes almost all beverage containers, paints and empty paint containers, flammable liquids, lead acid batteries, used motor oil, oil filters, oil containers, automobile and light truck tires, pharmaceuticals, and electronics. Product manufacturers submit plans indicating how they will achieve required recovery rates and how they will pay for consumer collection systems, which consist of depots located across the province. British Columbia boasts a 50 percent diversion rate, meaning that one-half of the province's MSW never reaches the disposal system.[15]

In the European Union, car manufacturers must have achieved a recycling rate of 80 percent by weight by January 1, 2006, and the target for 2015 is 85 percent. The European Union also required that all Member States recycle at least 55 percent of packaging waste by the end of 2008. Even before the European Union established its waste packaging directive, Germany had established in 1991 its famous "Green Dot" packaging take-back program. This system has reduced the amount of packaging used: between 1991 and 1998 packaging consumption per capita decreased from 94.7 kg to 82.0 kg, albeit at the cost of €1.8 billion per year. South Korea has recently established extended producer responsibility programs for a variety of items.[16]

The kinds of programs enacted in the EU vary widely among Member States, and they include extended *product* responsibility as well as extended *producer* responsibility. Extended product responsibility programs count on consumers and retailers to share some of the direct burdens, whereas extended producer responsibility programs place the largest burden of internalizing product waste costs on the manufacturer. The philosophy underlying extended product and producer responsibility systems is similar: the polluter should pay to clean up waste rather than foist it on society at large. There are arguments in favor of both systems because consumers and producers alike contribute to the pollution created through consumer products. On the one hand, computer manufacturers, for example, have designed many toxic materials into their products, including lead, mercury, chromium, and PCBs. On the other hand, consumers buy these products and then throw them away, where the toxic materials can leach into surrounding groundwater and surface waters.

The amount of potential contamination associated with electronic waste is enormous. By one estimate, there were 632,000 pounds of mercury in computers discarded in the United States between 1997 and 2007. By contrast, 96,000 pounds of mercury are emitted every year from power plants, which are the largest remaining source of airborne mercury in the U.S. and whose emissions are high enough to warrant Clean Air Act regulations. Electronic devices like computers, cell phones, and televisions pose a special threat to human health and the environment. Many such products fail the EPA chemical test that distinguishes hazardous from non-hazardous wastes, meaning that they would have to be managed at hazardous waste sites, were it not for the exception that allows all household waste to be disposed at municipal waste landfills.[17]

Because of the unique dangers that they pose, electronic devices and products containing household hazardous waste should be among the first regulated under a national scheme in the United States. There are many possible policy approaches, including the advance recycling fee and producer responsibility schemes employed in Alberta and British Columbia that were described above. As of July 1, 2006, the European Union has forbidden the sale of new electronic products with certain toxic components. The United States would be well served to follow the European Union's example, especially since many of the same computer companies whose products must now meet the EU's specifications sell similar products in the United States. Regulatory restrictions on hazardous components should be complemented by a national consumer tax on electronic products that could be returned to the states for use in setting up collection and recycling systems.[18]

For components of the MSW stream without hazardous materials we should make the costs of trash generation and disposal more visible, so that we all have an incentive to reduce the amount of waste we generate. Sending less MSW to landfills should have the salutary side effect of decreasing the amount of MSW transported over long distances for burial. Of course, to the extent that consumers, businesses, and government agencies respond to variable trash pricing by placing more items in recycling bins, that will increase the amount of materials transported to recycling facilities. But the latter use is more justifiable than is sending recyclable MSW to landfills, since in recycling we reuse an item rather than simply bury it in the ground, where its potential productive value lies unused and where eventually it becomes a contaminant. Recycling has substantial benefits, including reduced greenhouse gas emissions, reducing pollution and conserving resources, jobs creation, stimulating green technologies, and diverting waste from landfills and incinerators.[19]

While many efforts have been made in U.S. cities, towns, and states to reduce MSW generation, there is no overarching national program that requires waste diversion from landfills or waste reduction, and the time has come to craft a national program that fosters these two interrelated goals. The United States has a strong legacy of leaving trash collection and disposal to local and state governments, who, in turn, increasingly contract with private companies for those services. In a country as vast as the United States it makes sense to continue to rely on a federalized system with a strong private component. Decentralization also allows for local experimentation, which has yielded many valuable practical lessons. But it also makes sense to broaden waste-reduction efforts by strengthening the national government's role.

The European Union has established some useful waste diversion program examples that could be adapted to the UnitedStates' setting. The European Union's directives on reducing waste are expressed in the form of percentage diversion goals and EU Member States are responsible for deciding how to best meet those goals, given their individual circumstances. For example, to divert 65 percent of biodegradable waste from landfills, Member States might choose to undertake aggressive public education efforts about composting, they might impose variable pricing for biodegradable MSW, they might place special containers at curbside for paper or for kitchen waste, they might fine waste generators who place biodegradable waste in their trash cans, or they might undertake some combination of these approaches.

This same overall framework makes sense in the United States for MSW like paper, organic kitchen wastes, and other non-hazardous components of the MSW stream like bottles and cans. A set of national waste diversion goals should be established, and each state should be responsible for setting forth its plans for meeting those goals. Those goals should be based upon analytical studies undertaken by EPA, they should draw on the experiences of American states and municipalities and those of other countries, and they should reward state and local governments who have already forged ahead in this arena with early reduction credits.

Implementing a set of national waste diversion goals might not reduce the overall amount of MSW produced. Consumers and businesses will likely react to waste diversion goals by segregating recyclable and reusable wastes from trash destined for disposal, but there is no guarantee that they will change their consumption habits so as to produce less unwanted stuff that needs to go "away." Still, many businesses, government agencies, and individuals may find that, when they look closely, certain kinds of waste are unnecessary and that physical waste is a manifestation of inefficiencies that can and should be eliminated. Perhaps merely by encouraging more waste diversion consumers and businesses will be encouraged to respond by reducing the overall amount of MSW produced.

The EPA should be charged with conducting a broad study that analyzes the costs and benefits of regulatory efforts to reduce major portions of the waste stream like packaging. The results of that study should be used to design a national program to reduce the amount of MSW generated. The policy tools employed in that program could include market-based tools like green taxes.

By implementing a multi-pronged national effort to increase diversion, reduction, and recycling rates and to regulate and tax the disposal of electronic devices and household hazardous waste, which pose special hazards to human health and the environment, the overall amount of trash transported to, and disposed in, landfills will decrease. A national scheme with these goals will apply evenly across the country and it will build in large part on the many experiments that have already been undertaken by government authorities and private companies. As such, this approach builds on a stronger policy foundation and it will be easier to administer than myriad state laws to constrain the movement of trash across state lines.

Policy Solution II: Environmental Justice and the Proximity Principle

No one wants trash disposal sites near their home. While this sentiment has been disparaged as NIMBYism, in point of fact, it is a perfectly rational reaction to the introduction of a major source of pollution.[20] Even when properly managed, landfills and incinerators can cause adverse health effects, destroy wildlife habitat, and depress property values. At the same time, we need well-built, carefully monitored landfills because as a nation we generate almost 254 million tons of MSW annually. Even if we manage to divert and reduce generated waste substantially, we will still need many landfills and incinerators distributed across the country.

State and local officials have often reacted differently to our continuing need for waste disposal capacity and the trend toward huge, regional landfills. State officials regularly claim that waste transported from other states fills up "their" landfill capacity, but local government authorities generally hold the power to decide whether or not to allow landfills in their communities. And, as we have seen, many such authorities have decided to trade the use of local land for the revenue received from landfills.

A federally imposed garbage tax can partially resolve the struggle between state governments, who wish to minimize environmental contamination and the costs thereof, and local authorities, who often turn to trash as the only viable source of revenues for underfunded public services. Federal law requires that MSW landfill operators conduct "post-closure care" for thirty years after a landfill stops accepting waste.[21] However, many landfills may create environmental problems even after thirty years have elapsed.

As such, the federal government should impose uniform taxes on every ton of trash disposed, no matter where that garbage comes from. Such a tax could range from $1 per ton to $5 per ton, which is a small fraction of current disposal fees—average regional tipping fees in 2005 ranged from $24.50 per ton in the central U.S. to $70.53 per ton in the northeastern U.S.—and represents a charge nationwide of only a few dollars per year per person. If even small fees in this range were imposed on every ton of MSW generated in the U.S., this fund would grow by hundreds of millions of dollars annually. These monies would be used for environmental stewardship—for example, to mitigate present and future contamination and to subsidize recycling and waste-reduction programs. In Virginia as elsewhere, a given amount of trash from New York City has the same potential to harm surrounding surface waters as does the same amount from Charlottesville, Virginia. Thus, it is sensible to impose a tax on both in-state and out-of-state waste generators. Taxes also force consumers to pay for more of MSW's responsibility for MSW management and its social and environmental consequences.

States could be allowed to impose their own trash taxes and to escalate those taxes as a function of how far the trash travels from its point of origin, thereby providing a disincentive to long-distance transport. The revenue from these taxes should be shared with local governments who might experience lower landfill revenues as a result of the tax. Since such taxes would be based on the distance trash travels, they are less likely to run afoul of the Commerce Clause. For example, under such a system, trash traveling from central New Jersey to nearby eastern Pennsylvania might be taxed less than trash traveling hundreds of miles from western Pennsylvania to eastern Pennsylvania, and, similarly, garbage imported from North Carolina to southeastern Virginia might be taxed less than trash moving from northern Virginia to southern Virginia.

Some trash-importing states are already turning to the idea of tonnage-based environmental fees, with variable success. Trash fee proposals have been introduced several times over the past decade in Virginia, but none has been enacted into law. In contrast with Virginia, the Commonwealth of Pennsylvania has adopted a trash disposal fee of $7.25 per ton, to be implemented in stages. This tax applies to all trash disposed in the Commonwealth, and the funds collected will be used for various environmentally oriented purposes—for example, to clean up rivers and streams and to finance recycling programs.

It is possible that some companies have already chosen to avoid Pennsylvania's tax by sending their waste elsewhere. MSW imports to Pennsylvania declined by 1.6 million tons annually, or 21 percent overall, between 2000 and 2005, and more than one-third of that decline occurred between 2004 and 2005, after the first stage of the fee ($4/ton) was adopted in 2002. This decrease happened even as trash transport generally has steadily risen. In contrast with the situation in Pennsylvania, Virginia's imported MSW rose by 2.3 million tons per year between 2001 and 2007.[22]

We should go beyond trying to discourage the long-distance transport of MSW and ensure that landfill or incinerator host communities, despite their racial or income profiles, receive fair treatment with respect to all important aspects of MSW management—for example, frequency of enforcement inspections and compensation from the landfill companies. EPA should establish local empowerment offices to educate the general public on the environmental effects of disposal facilities and help affected citizens become meaningfully involved in the public decision-making process when a landfill or incinerator is under consideration, during the process of deciding where to site the facility, as the facility is permitted, and as that facility's operation is overseen by state and local authorities. The professional staff of these offices could be contractors to EPA, to ensure their independence of state or local political pressures.

EPA should develop for these local empowerment offices a checklist of public access and education procedures that must be followed when MSW disposal facilities are under consideration and when they are in operation. These procedures should ensure that affected citizens can have meaningful input. Much as the Superfund program awards Technical Assistance Grants to citizens and communities so they can hire consultants, this program should also fund outside experts who can provide guidance for citizens in affected communities. All information communicated by the empowerment offices and by the experts must be communicated in laymen's terms, so that its meaning is transparent to members of the general public.

Finally, genuine political empowerment should be complemented by fair economic compensation for present and future generations. The federal government should issue guidelines for local communities to help them determine a fair landfill host fee. Landfill hosts should share in the potential benefits of the landfill, such as the generation of energy from landfill methane, which more and more waste companies are undertaking.

As a mechanism for instituting these new procedures, EPA should revise its requirements for state MSW management plans. In their plans, states should also be required to describe how they are anticipating their citizens' MSW disposal needs and to discuss how they will avoid concentrating landfills and incinerators in certain geographic areas. One possibility would be to ask each state to set a limit on the number of MSW disposal sites that can be located in a given area.[23]

In thinking about how to protect local communities from unfair treatment, it makes sense to consider the potential applicability of the proximity principle in the U.S. The EU's policies establish a high hurdle for MSW to cross Member State lines for disposal, but MSW that will be recycled or burned for energy recovery is considered beneficial trade that is not restricted in any way. The ultimate expression of the proximity principle is found in Japan, where the central government has financed many landfills and incinerators in virtually *everyone*'s back yard, with the express purpose of ensuring that waste does not travel far from genera- tion to disposal. This policy has had a startling effect on the number of disposal units in Japan. In 2002 there were 1,490 incinerators and 2,047 MSW landfills in Japan, a country with a population of 127 million and an annual MSW stream of 51.6 million Mg per year. By comparison, the U.S. in 2002 served a total population of 288 million generating 213 million Mg of MSW with only 107 incinerators and 1,767 landfills. One observer claims that Japan is home to approximately 70 percent of the world's MSW incinerators.[24]

Japan's investment in so many facilities implies inefficiency and high costs. Average disposal costs in Japan are approximately $400/ton, ex- ceeding by an order of magnitude those in the United States, which rose very little between 1995 and 2004 and averaged $34/ton in 2004. On the one hand, this has added urgency to recycling, and the Japanese are now leaders in that arena. On the other hand, sprinkling waste management facilities widely increases the population at risk of exposure to environ- mental pollution associated with MSW disposal practices. Despite the central importance of the proximity principle in Japan, escalating costs and dioxin emissions from small incinerators have driven many munici- palities to join forces and to invest in regional incinerators.[25]

On constitutional, geographic, and economic grounds it does not make sense in the United States to embrace the proximity principle in Japanese fashion, which involves a great deal of central government control. The United States' federal system acknowledges that state and local governments have powers independent of the national govern-

Curbside recycling in Japan. (Photo courtesy of Itaru Okuda)

ment. In keeping with this tradition, the national government does not instruct local or state governments on whether they may or may not accept specific kinds of land uses as long as those uses comply with federal regulations, for example, Clean Air Act incineration rules.[26]

While Japan's policy version of the proximity principle is not transferable to the U.S. setting, state-imposed escalator taxes that penalize long-distance transport could help provide incentives for disposal closer to the trash's point of origin. Flow control ordinances attempt to manage trash locally and thus they represent a version of the proximity principle. To the extent that municipalities implement flow control but do not interfere with the flow of interstate commerce, such efforts should be regarded as constructive examples of ways to keep trash at home.

We should investigate the feasibility, costs, and benefits of implementing some version of the EU's proximity principle in the U.S. The European Union's version of the proximity principle holds that Member States should dispose of their MSW within their own borders but that they may engage in unrestricted international trade of MSW intended for recycling or energy recovery. Individual Member States undertake to develop their own individualized MSW programs, as long as they adhere to the EU's laws and overarching principles. Some U.S. cities have already recognized the perverseness and inefficiencies involved with sending MSW hundreds of miles away for disposal. For example, New York City aims to divert 70 percent of its MSW from landfill disposal by 2015.

Taking Responsibility for Trash

In this book I have sought to understand whether it makes sense to allow states to constrain the movement of trash across their borders. I conclude that the policy problems associated with trash transport have little to do with movement across state borders. While state officials are right to worry about the environmental contamination that will result from mega-landfills, barriers to MSW imports erected by one state will only deflect the waste to others. And such shifts would deprive landfill host communities of tax revenue, which some need badly because their state governments do not provide generous support for basic public services like schools.

Millions of tons of garbage traverse hundreds of miles along American highways, rails, and waterways for the following reasons: we make a lot of trash; constructing and maintaining modern, environmentally protective landfills and incinerators is expensive, and thus their operators have increasingly built huge regional facilities that can attract enough trash to make them financially viable; and it is difficult to site new disposal facilities, which tend to be located in rural areas that are economically and politically vulnerable. The levels of pollution that will emanate from mega-landfills are worrisome and the current system of siting landfills should be fairer and more protective of communities hosting waste disposal facilities.

To remedy this array of problems we should: set national goals for decreasing MSW production; increase waste diversion and recycling; regulate the disposal of electronic devices, since they contain especially hazardous compounds; institute new political protections through the RCRA solid waste planning process for potential or actual host communities, so that they can make fully informed decisions and so they will receive fair compensation if they consent to having a waste facility; require states to integrate into their solid waste plans measures for taking care of their citizens' solid waste needs and for avoiding areas with unusually highly concentrated numbers of MSW operations; and establish a federally imposed garbage tax that would be collected at disposal facilities and redistributed to state and local governments.

Those revenues will provide funds for environmental cleanup, they can be used to support waste prevention and recycling, and the tax will give waste generators everywhere reason to reduce their MSW generation. States could be allowed to impose "escalator" taxes that would rise as a function of how far the trash travels, thereby providing a disincentive to long-distance transport. A portion of such escalator taxes should be redistributed to local governments whose landfill or incinerator revenues fall as a result of the tax.

These solutions recognize that trash is inevitably both a commodity and pollution. To the extent that Americans want to continue to have trash taken "away," someone must be paid for the associated collection and disposal services. Thus the commercial aspects of trash are natural and unavoidable. But like all pollution, trash does not really go "away." It moves into someone's back yard, and there it contaminates the air, land, and water. Following the example of our counterparts in the EU and Japan, and building on the policy leadership of many U.S. cities and towns, as a nation we must take greater responsibility for the amount of trash we generate and for its adverse impacts on human health and the environment. In so doing we will solve the real problems with long-distance trash transport.

Notes

Introduction

1. Davis, *When Smoke Ran Like Water;* McDonough and Braungart, *Cradle to Cradle.*

2. Buddy Duseau, trash hauler, interview, in Schwerin and Schwerin, *Talking Trash.*

3. U.S. Environmental Protection Agency, "Methane: Sources and Emissions"; Thorneloe, *U.S. EPA's Field Test Programs;* Christenson and Cozzarelli, *Norman Landfill Environmental Research Site.*

4. Verchick, "Commerce Clause"; U.S. Congressional Research Service, *Interstate Shipment of MSW: 2007 Update.*

5. "New York v. Virginia: Dumping Grounds," *The Economist,* February 20, 1999, 27; U.S. Congressional Research Service, *Interstate Shipment of MSW: 2007 Update.*

6. Griffin, "Garbage Crisis"; Nosenchuck, "25th Anniversary of the New York State Department of Environmental Conservation"; Miller, *Fat of the Land.*

7. Lipton, "As Imported Garbage Piles Up, So Do Worries"; Lipton, "City Trash Follows Long and Winding Road"; "Reciprocal Garbage," *New York Post,* January 15, 1999; Vivian E. Thomson, interview by Amy Scott, "Turning Trash into Cash," *Marketplace,* American Public Media broadcast, November 9, 2007, http://marketplace .publicradio.org/display/web/2007/11/09/consumed2_mm_7/.

8. Speth, *Red Sky at Morning;* Diamond, *Collapse.*

1. All Garbage Is Local

1. Martin Tolchin, "Thomas P. O'Neill Jr., A Democratic Power in the House for Decades, Dies at 81," *New York Times,* January 7, 1995.

2. Melosi, *Garbage in the Cities.*

3. Thomson and White, "Garbage In, Garbage Out."

4. Mike Giuranna, Solid Waste Specialist, U.S. Environmental Protection Agency, Region 3, to author, October 11, 2005.

5. U.S. Environmental Protection Agency, "Municipal Solid Waste, 2007."

6. As reported in Murray and Spence, "Fair Weather Federalism," 74.

7. U.S. Environmental Protection Agency, "Municipal Solid Waste, 2007."

8. U.S. Environmental Protection Agency, "Methane: Sources and Emissions"; U.S. Department of Health and Human Services, "Landfill Gas Primer"; Eklund et al., "Landfill Gas at Fresh Kills."

9. El-Fadel et al., "Environmental Impacts of Solid Waste Landfilling."

10. U.S. Environmental Protection Agency, "Landfill Methane Outreach Program," http://www.epa.gov/lmop/overview.htm.

11. Okuda and Thomson, "Regionalization in Japan"; Integrated Waste Services, "Fact Sheet."

12. U.S. Environmental Protection Agency, "Air Regulations for Municipal Waste Combustors."

13. Sabbas et al., "Municipal Solid Waste Incineration Residues"; Puder, "Trash, Ash, and the Phoenix"; Astrup et al., "Towards an Improved Understanding of Leaching Behavior."

14. El-Fadel et al., "Environmental Impacts of Solid Waste Landfilling"; Knickerbocker, "Katrina Lays Bare Superfund Woes."

15. These regulations are codified in the Code of Federal Regulations, Title 40, Part 258 ("Criteria for Municipal Solid Waste Landfills"), http://www.access.gpo.gov/nara/cfr/waisidx_03/40cfr258_03.html; New York State's MSW landfill regulations are described at http://www.dec.ny.gov/chemical/23682.html.

16. Puder, "Trash, Ash, and the Phoenix."

17. Sources of information for statistics cited in this section are U.S. Congressional Research Service, *Managing Electronic Waste;* U.S. Government Accountability Office, "Electronic Waste"; Mooallem, "Afterlife of Cell Phones"; U.S. Environmental Protection Agency, "Management of Electronic Wastes."

18. Solid Waste Disposal Act as Amended Through Public Law 107-377, Public Law 94-580, 107th Cong., 2d sess. (December 31, 2002), 81–82.

19. U.S. Environmental Protection Agency, "FY 2008: EPA Budget in Brief."

20. Montgomery, "Effects of the Loma Prieta Earthquake"; Strasser, *Waste and Want;* Melosi, *Garbage in the Cities;* Louis, "Historical Context of Municipal Solid Waste."

21. California Integrated Waste Management Board, "Waste Banned from the Trash," http://www.ciwmb.ca.gov/HHW/Info/default.htm.

22. U.S. Congressional Research Service, *Interstate Shipment of MSW: 2004 Update;* U.S. Environmental Protection Agency, "Assessment of OSW's 35 Percent MSW Goal"; Adam B. Ellick, "Houston Resists Recycling and Independent Streak Is Cited," *New York Times,* July 29, 2008.

23. Canterbury and Newill, "Pay-As-You-Throw Payoff."

24. U.S. Congressional Research Service, *Managing Electronic Waste;* U.S. Congressional Research Service, *Interstate Shipment of MSW: 2007 Update.*

25. U.S. Environmental Protection Agency, "Municipal Solid Waste, 2006"; Repa, "Solid Waste Disposal Trends." According to Repa, Texas, Virginia, Wisconsin, and Alaska reported 748, 256, 727, and 404 closures, respectively; no other state reported more than 200 closures.

26. Griffin, "Garbage Crisis"; Lipton, "As Imported Garbage Piles Up, So Do Worries."

27. Repa, "Solid Waste Disposal Trends"; Repa, "Interstate Movement of Solid Waste"; U.S. Government Accounting Office, "Hazardous and Non-Hazardous Waste."

28. As of this writing, Allied Waste and Republic Services were poised to merge. Thomson and White, "Garbage In, Garbage Out"; Repa, "Interstate Movement of Solid Waste."

29. Duffy, "Landfill Macroeconomics"; Duffy, "Landfill Economics Part II"; Jeff Bailey, "Waste Yes, Want Not: Rumors of a Shortage of Dump Space Were Greatly Exaggerated," *New York Times*, August 12, 2005.

30. Virginia General Assembly, "Solid Waste Management Facilities"; Paul Schwartzman, "New York City Garbage a Mixed Bag," *New York Daily News*, January 25, 1999; McGovern, *Campo Indian Landfill War.*

31. New York City Department of City Planning, "Fresh Kills Park Project"; Verchick, "Commerce Clause"; Rathje and Murphy, *Rubbish;* Melosi, *Garbage in the Cities.*

32. Blaine Harden, "Trade Trash for Culture? Not Virginia," *New York Times*, January 18, 1999; Lipton, "As Imported Garbage Piles Up, So Do Worries"; Vivian E. Thomson, interview by Amy Scott, "Turning Trash into Cash," *Marketplace*, American Public Media broadcast, November 9, 2007, http://marketplace.publicradio .org/display/web/2007/11/09/consumed2_mm_7/; Royte, *Garbage Land.*

33. U.S. Constitution, Art. 1, sec. 8, cl. 3.

34. *Pike v. Bruce Church, Inc.*, 397 U.S. 137 (1970); *City of Philadelphia v. New Jersey*, 437 U.S. 617, 624 (1978).

35. *Chemical Waste Management, Inc. v. Hunt*, 504 U.S. 332 (1992); *Fort Gratiot Sanitary Landfill, Inc. v. Michigan Department of Natural Resources*, 504 U.S. 332 (1992); *Oregon Waste Systems, Inc. v. Department of Environmental Quality of Oregon*, 511 U.S. 93 (1994). The Court decided the first two cases on the same day.

36. *C. A. Carbone v. Town of Clarkstown*, 511 U.S. 383 (1994); Nosenchuck, "25th Anniversary of the New York State Department of Environmental Conservation"; U.S. Senate Committee on Environment and Public Works, *Transportation and Flow Control of Solid Waste.*

37. *Waste Management Holdings v. Gilmore*, 252 F.3d 316 (4th Cir. 2001).

38. *United Haulers Association v. Oneida-Herkimer Solid Waste Management Authority*, 127 S.Ct. 1786, 1795 (2007).

39. U.S. Congressional Research Service, *Interstate Trash Transport;* U.S. Congressional Research Service, *Solid Waste Issues in the 106th Congress;* U.S. Congressional Research Service, *Interstate Shipment of MSW: 2004 Update.*

40. Ursery, "Kerry Vows to Ban Canadian Imports."

41. Merrill, "Golden Rules for Transboundary Pollution."

2. WASTE NOT, WANT NOT

1. The data comparison in this chapter relies heavily on the work of Dr. Itaru Okuda, who translated Japanese documents and reinterpreted the Japanese data to make them comparable with those of the United States and the European Union.

2. Colonel Waring, commissioner of street cleaning from 1895 to 1896, exhorted New Yorkers to separate their trash so that the ash, a large component of household waste at the time, could be reused (Strasser, *Waste and Want,* 128).

3. Ibid., 201.

4. Packard, *Waste Makers,* 183.

5. Thompson, *Rubbish Theory;* Grossman and Krueger, "Economic Growth and the Environment."

6. Schumacher, *Small Is Beautiful;* Daly, *Beyond Growth;* Ehrlich and Ehrlich, "Population Explosion"; Melosi, *Garbage in the Cities.*

7. Grossman, "Pollution and Growth."

8. Hussen, *Principles of Environmental Economics;* Beckerman, *Small Is Stupid.*

9. Grossman, "Pollution and Growth," 22.

10. Yardley, "China's Next Big Boom"; Kahn and Yardley, "As China Roars, Pollution Reaches Deadly Extremes."

11. Simon, "Upheaval in the East"; Wines, "Malawi Is Burning."

12. Davis, *When Smoke Ran Like Water;* Crenson, *Un-politics of Air Pollution.* According to Bruce Grant, a biologist at the College of William and Mary, although the peppered moth research has been questioned and reinterpreted, its basic lessons remain intact; see http://www.millerandlevine.com/km/evol/Moths/grant-pratt-tribune.html.

13. Grossman, "Pollution and Growth"; Grossman and Krueger, "Economic Growth and the Environment"; Selden et al., "Analyzing the Reductions in U.S. Air Pollution"; Rothman and de Bruyn, "Probing into the Environmental Kuznets Curve Hypothesis."

14. U.S. Environmental Protection Agency, *Acid Rain: 2006 Progress Report.* On July 11, 2008, the Clean Air Interstate Rule was vacated; see *State of North Carolina v. United States Environmental Protection Agency,* 531 F.3d 896 (D.C. Cir. 2008). On October 21, 2008, the D.C. Circuit asked the parties to submit briefings in the CAIR litigation, which may mean that the court may stay its mandate until EPA revises the rule.

15. European Environment Agency, *Europe's Environment: The Fourth Assessment,* chapter 6; Kahn and Landler, "China Grabs West's Smoke-Spewing Factories"; Rothman, "Environmental Kuznets Curve"; Grossman, "Pollution and Growth."

16. Rothman and de Bruyn, "Probing into the Environmental Kuznets Curve Hypothesis"; Baldwin, "Does Sustainability Require Growth?"; Selden et al., "Analyzing the Reductions in U.S. Air Pollution."

17. Hussen, *Principles of Environmental Economics;* World Bank, *World Development Report 1992.*

18. This section, which examines the empirical relationship between per capita generation of MSW and per capita GDP, relies on research done jointly with Dr. Itaru Okuda, who has provided unique access to, and analysis of, Japanese documents on MSW generation; see Okuda and Thomson, "Regionalization in Japan"; Thomson and Okuda, "Garbage In, Garbage Out."

19. Nemat Shafik, "Economic Development and Environmental Quality." The

EU-15 Member States are Austria, Belgium, Denmark, Finland, France, Germany, Greece, Ireland, Italy, Luxembourg, the Netherlands, Portugal, Spain, Sweden, and the United Kingdom. The EU-12 Member States are Bulgaria, Croatia, the Czech Republic, Estonia, Hungary, Latvia, Lithuania, Malta, Poland, Romania, Slovenia, and Slovakia. The comparison of average MSW generated in the EU-15 and EU-12 is based on 2005 data from the European Environment Agency (see "Municipal Waste Generated Per Capita, 1995–2005"). For the survey of literature on income and MSW generated, see Mazzanti et al., "Municipal Waste Generation and Socio-economic Drivers." Mazzanti et al. define "value added" as the incremental component of wealth attributed to the geographical area.

20. Melosi, *Garbage in the Cities.*

21. Organisation for Economic Cooperation and Development, "OECD Factbook 2007: Economic, Environmental, and Social Statistics," graph of MSW waste generation.

22. Thomson and Okuda, "Garbage In, Garbage Out."

23. U.S. Environmental Protection Agency, "Assessment of OSW's 35 Percent MSW Goal"; European Environment Agency, *Europe's Environment: Third Assessment,* chapter 7; Okuda and Thomson, "Regionalization in Japan."

24. U.S. Environmental Protection Agency, "Municipal Solid Waste, 2006"; Simmons et al., "State of Garbage in America."

25. Simmons et al., "State of Garbage in America." See also Kaufman et al., "State of Garbage in America"; Miller, "Losing Count."

26. Shelly Schneider, Franklin Associates, to author, July 22, 2005, citing a study completed by the Oregon Department of Environmental Quality.

27. European Environment Agency, "Municipal Waste Generated Per Capita, 1995–2005."

28. All data except those of Simmons et al. apply to the year 2002, as this is the year most easily compared. For the United States and the EU-15 Member States, 2002 data do not differ substantially from data reported for more recent years. More recent data for Japan were not available.

29. Onishi, "How Do Japanese Dump Trash?"; Okuda and Thomson, "Regionalization in Japan."

30. King County, Washington, "2006 Solid Waste Division Annual Report."

31. Ursery, "Aiming High"; San Francisco Department of Solid Waste, *Building a Bright Future.*

32. European Environment Agency, "Municipal Waste Generated Per Capita, 1995–2005"; Vandeputte, "Waste Management, Planning, and Results in Flanders."

33. The source of data for the United States and the EU Member States is European Environment Agency, "Municipal Waste Generated Per Capita, 1995–2005"; U.S. Environmental Protection Agency, "Municipal Solid Waste, 2007."

34. U.S. Environmental Protection Agency, "Recycling Is Working"; Ackerman, *Why Do We Recycle?*

35. To facilitate comparisons with Japan, the data presented in figure 1 are from 2002.

36. U.S. Environmental Protection Agency, "Municipal Solid Waste, 2007."

37. These statements are based on the observations of Dr. Itaru Okuda. The 2004 recycling and MSW data are from European Commission, *Europe in Figures: Eurostat Yearbook, 2006–7,* and U.S. Environmental Protection Agency, "Municipal Solid Waste, 2007."

38. Okuda, "State of Waste Management in Japan"; Onorato, "Japanese Recycling Law Takes Effect"; Onishi, "How Do the Japanese Dump Trash?"

39. European Environment Agency, *Waste: Annual Topic Update 1998;* European Environment Agency, *Environment in the EU at the Turn of the Century,* chapter 3.7. U.S. figures were calculated using table 18 of U.S. Environmental Protection Agency, "Characterization of Municipal Solid Waste: 1996 Update," which reports that Americans disposed of 11,530,000 tons of glass containers in 1995. This figure was converted to kilograms (10,480,000,000 kg) and was then divided by the U.S. Census Bureau's estimate that the U.S. population in 1995 was 261,638,000 (U.S. Census Bureau, "Population Profile of the United States: 1995"). Tables 15 and 18 of this same EPA report show that in 1995 Americans generated 43,550,000 tons of paper waste in the "non-durable" goods category, and 38,080,000 tons of paper packaging waste. These figures, when added and converted to kilograms, indicate that Americans generated 74,209,000,000 kg of paper waste in 1995, for a per capita rate of 285 kg annually.

40. U.S. Department of State, "Background Note: Luxembourg," http://www .state.gov/r/pa/ei/bgn/3182.htm (accessed February 23, 2008).

41. U.S. Environmental Protection Agency, "Municipal Solid Waste, 2007," table 19; U.S. Environmental Protection Agency, "Materials Generated in the Municipal Waste Stream," table 18; U.S. Environmental Protection Agency, "Characterization of Municipal Solid Waste: 1996 Update," table 24; *Park, "Casemakers Converted* to the Lighter Side*"; Business Services Industry, '*The Aluminum Association Says Americans Recycle 2 of 3 Aluminum Cans," April 19, 2001, http://findarticles .com/p/articles/mi_moEIN/is_2001_April_19/ai_73400494.

42. U.S. Census Bureau, "USA Quick Facts"; U.S. Census Bureau, "Your Gateway to Census 2000"; U.S. Department of Commerce, Bureau of Economic Analysis, "National Income and Product Accounts Tables"; U.S. Environmental Protection Agency, "Materials Generated in the Municipal Waste Stream."

43. Kahn and Landler, "China Grabs West's Smoke-Spewing Factories"; Mark Landler, "East Germany Is Able to Prevent Industrial Flight to Third World," *New York Times,* November 21, 2003; European Environment Agency, *Environmental Outlook: Municipal Waste;* European Environment Agency, "Municipal Waste Generation—Assessment Published January 2008."

44. European Environment Agency, *Environmental Outlook: Municipal Waste.* The EU-10 Member Nations are Cyprus, the Czech Republic, Estonia, Hungary, Latvia, Lithuania, Malta, Poland, Slovakia, and Slovenia.

45. Repa, "NSWMA's 2005 Tip Fee Survey"; European Environment Agency, *Waste: Annual Topic Update 1998;* Japan data are from Okuda and Thomson, "Regionalization in Japan"; Italy data are from European Environment Bureau, "Qual-

ity of Implementation of the Waste Landfill Directive"; Flanders data are from Rudy Meeus, director, Flanders Waste Agency; Denmark and Netherlands data are from European Environment Agency, "Country Fact Sheets on Waste Management"; Germany data are from Elisabeth Rosenthal, "A Whiff of Naples Is Arriving in Hamburg," *New York Times*, June 9, 2008.

46. Barber, *Con $umed;* Whybrow, *American Mania;* David Brooks, "The Culture of Debt," *New York Times*, July 22, 2008; Jared Diamond, "What's Your Consumption Factor?" *New York Times*, January 2, 2008.

47. Schor, *Overspent American*, chapter 1. See also Kiger, "Living Ever Larger."

48. Harvey, "Comparison of Household Saving Ratios."

49. Organisation for Economic Cooperation and Development, "OECD Factbook 2007: Economic, Environmental, and Social Statistics."

50. U.S. Department of Labor, "Consumer Expenditures in 2002." Average per capita spending was computed by dividing "consumer unit" expenditure by 2.5, the average number of persons per consumer unit (see ibid., table A). For the European statistics, see 2002 statistics in European Environment Agency, *Household Consumption and the Environment*. Euro-to-dollar conversion employs the exchange rate as of December 31, 2002, or 1.0487 dollars to the euro. Food consumption statistics are drawn from U.S. Department of Agriculture, Economic Research Service, *Average Daily Per Capita Calories;* and from UN Food and Agriculture Organization, *FAO Statistical Yearbook, 2005–2006*, table D-1. The FAO defines "food consumption" as "the amount of food available for human consumption as estimated by the FAO Food Balance Sheets," with this caveat: "However the actual food consumption may be lower than the quantity shown as food availability depending on the magnitude of wastage and losses of food in the household, e.g. during storage, in preparation and cooking, as plate-waste or quantities fed to domestic animals and pets, thrown or given away" (see http://www.fao.org/es/ess/faostat/foodsecurity/FSSDMetadata_en.htm).

51. Okuda and Thomson, "Regionalization in Japan"; U.S. Congressional Research Service, *Managing Electronic Waste;* U.S. Congressional Research Service, *Interstate Shipment of MSW: 2007 Update.*

52. Okuda and Thomson, "Regionalization in Japan."

53. European Commission, *EU Focus on Waste Management.*

54. European Environment Agency, *Europe's Environment: Fourth Assessment.* For more details on these directives, see the European Commission's website at http://ec.europa.eu/environment/waste/index.htm.

55. U.S. Environmental Protection Agency, "Materials Generated in the Municipal Waste Stream"; European Commission, *Waste Prevention and Minimisation;* European Environment Agency, *Europe's Environment: Third Assessment*, chapter 7; Sarah Lyall, "Laws Tell Britons Exactly How to Take Out Trash," *New York Times*, June 27, 2008; Duales System Deutschland GmbH, "DSD GmbH Looks Back in [sic] 17 Successful Years," October 4, 2007, http://www.gruener-punkt.de/index.php?id=1785&L=1.

56. Jacques Hoffenberg, Consultant to Waste Denmark, interview by author, December 6, 2007, Brussels, Belgium.

57. I am indebted to Rudy Meeus, director, OVAM, and Philippe van de Velde, also of OVAM, Mechelen, Belgium, for providing the information and data cited here and below.

3. Costs and Benefits of Interstate Trash Transport

1. U.S. Environmental Protection Agency, "Municipal Solid Waste, 2006"; Repa, "Interstate Movement of Solid Waste."

2. U.S. Environmental Protection Agency, "Municipal Solid Waste, 2006"; New York Department of City Planning, "Fresh Kills Park Project"; Repa, "Interstate Movement of Solid Waste."

3. Repa, "Interstate Movement of Solid Waste"; New York Department of Environmental Conservation, "Solid Waste Management Facilities"; Virginia Department of Environmental Quality, "Solid Waste Managed in Virginia, 2006"; census data are the most recent available from the U.S. Census Bureau. New York State data taken from http://factfinder.census.gov/; Burnley, "Statement of Robert K. Burnley," 164.

4. Melosi, *Garbage in the Cities.*

5. Ibid.

6. Colten, "Chicago's Waste Lands"; Thale, "Waste Disposal"; Chicago Recycling Coalition, Chicago recycling timeline, http://www.chicagorecycling.org/index .php?option=com_content&task=view&id=24&Itemid=116; Pellow, *Garbage Wars.*

7. Colten, "Chicago's Waste Lands"; Thale, "Waste Disposal."

8. Virginia Department of Environmental Quality, "Municipal Solid Waste: Historical Review"; landfill capacity data obtained from Virginia Department of Environmental Quality, "Solid Waste Managed in Virginia, 2007," attachment 4. The MSW landfills in the central to southeast quadrant of Virginia are Atlantic Waste Disposal (Sussex County), BFI King and Queen (King and Queen County), BFI Old Dominion (City of Richmond), Brunswick Waste Management Facility (Brunswick County), Maplewood Recycling and Waste Disposal (Amelia County), Middle Peninsula Landfill (Gloucester County), Shoosmith Sanitary Landfill (Chesterfield County), SPSA (City of Suffolk), USA Waste of Virginia (City of Hampton), and Waste Management (Charles City County). Virginia Department of Environmental Quality, *Solid Waste Management Facilities in Virginia.*

9. Virginia Department of Environmental Quality, "Solid Waste Managed in Virginia, 2007"; Spar and Cai, *2005 Virginia Population Estimates.*

10. Thomas Jefferson Planning District, *Solid Waste Plan,* March 2008 (draft), http://www.tjpdc.org/pdf/Environment/SWMPrevised03-06-08.pdf.

11. New York City Department of City Planning, "Fresh Kills Park Project."

12. Quoted in U.S. Senate Committee on Environment and Public Works, *Interstate Waste and Flow Control,* http://epw.senate.gov/107th/Allan_032002.htm.

13. New York City Department of Sanitation, "Request for Expressions of Interest"; Winnie Hu, "Newly Approved Trash Plan Puts Emphasis on Recycling," *New York Times,* July 21, 2006; Sze, *Noxious New York,* 114; Angotti, "City's New Waste Plan"; Senate Committee on Environment and Public Works, *Interstate Waste and Flow Control.*

14. U.S. House Committee on Energy and Commerce, *Hearing before the Subcommittee on Environment and Hazardous Materials*, 103; South Carolina demographic data are from *http://www.fedstats.gov/qf/states/45/45061.html*.

15. Andrews, "Landfills: Host Fees"; Virginia Department of Environmental Quality, *Municipal Solid Waste: Historical Review;* Lipton, "Crackdown on Trucks Leaves Piles of Trash"; Virginia Department of Environmental Quality, "Solid Waste Managed in Virginia, 2007." Census statistics are the most recent available at http://quickfacts.census.gov/qfd/states/51/51036.html; Unnever et al., "District Variations."

16. Wallgren, "Town Meeting Rejects BFI Plan." East Bridgewater census data are from http://censtats.census.gov/data/MA/0602502318455.pdf. Brockton and Massachusetts data are from http://quickfacts.census.gov/qfd/states/25/2509000 .html.

17. Weegie Thompson, Waste Management, Inc., interview by Daniel Shean, n.d.; Virginia General Assembly, "Solid Waste Management Facilities," 10. For New York's and Virginia's regulations for MSW landfills, see, respectively, http://www .dec.ny.gov/regs/2491.html and http://leg1.state.va.us/cgi-bin/legp504.exe?000+ reg+9VAC20-80-250.

18. Repa, "NSWMA's 2005 Tip Fee Survey"; New York State Commission on Property Tax Relief, "Property Tax Relief," http://www.cptr.state.ny.us/ (accessed August 6, 2008); *New York Times*, "State-by-State Property Tax Rates," April 10, 2007.

19. U.S. General Accounting Office, *Siting of Hazardous Waste Landfills.*

20. Been, "Locally Undesirable Land Uses"; United Church of Christ, *Toxic Waste and Race in the United States.*

21. Bullard, *Dumping in Dixie;* Bullard and Wright, "Politics of Pollution"; Been, "Locally Undesirable Land Uses."

22. U.S. General Accounting Office, *Hazardous and Non-Hazardous Waste.*

23. Virginia General Assembly, "Solid Waste Management Facilities"; for Charles City County figures, see U.S. Census Bureau, "USA Quick Facts."

24. Virginia General Assembly, "Solid Waste Management Facilities," 73.

25. Ibid.

26. Faber and Krieg, "Unequal Exposure to Ecological Hazards," 281. Census statistics are from http://quickfacts.census.gov/qfd/states/25/2509000.html (Brockton and Massachusetts, 2006 estimates), and http://censtats.census.gov/ data/MA/1602509000.pdf (East Bridgewater, 2000 census data).

27. National Environmental Justice Advisory Council, *Regulatory Strategy.*

28. Rhodes, *Environmental Justice in America.*

29. This analysis draws on data compiled by Dan Shean, *Politics of Trash.*

30. Foreman, *Promise and Peril of Environmental Justice,* 27; Rhodes, *Environmental Justice in America;* Hird, *Superfund;* Ringquist, "Question of Justice"; Been, "Locally Undesirable Land Uses."

31. Suro, "Pollution-Weary Minorities Try Civil Rights Tack"; U.S. Centers for Disease Control, "Children at Risk from Ozone Air Pollution" and "Update: Blood

Lead Levels"; Been, "Locally Undesirable Land Uses"; Bullard, *Dumping in Dixie;* Hurley, *Environmental Inequalities;* Rhodes, *Environmental Justice in America;* Foreman, *Promise and Peril of Environmental Justice,* 83; Pellow, *Garbage Wars.*

32. Pulido, *Environmentalism and Economic Justice,* 13; McGovern, *Campo Indian Landfill War.*

33. Bullard, "Environmental Justice in the 21st Century," 445.

34. Summers, "Let Them Eat Pollution," 66.

35. Shrader-Frechette, *Environmental Justice.*

36. Ibid.; Shrader-Frechette, *Burying Uncertainty.*

37. Rhodes, *Environmental Justice in America,* 19; see also U.S. Environmental Protection Agency, Environmental Justice website, http://www.epa.gov/Complian ce/environmentaljustice/.

38. Foreman, *Promise and Peril of Environmental Justice,* 124.

4. Regulatory and Legislative Efforts to Limit the Movement of Trash

1. Melosi, *Garbage in the Cities.*

2. Pennsylvania DEP, "Amount of Waste Deposited in PA Landfills"; Specter, "Should States and Communities Be Allowed to Regulate Trash from Other States?"

3. *City of Philadelphia v. New Jersey,* 437 U.S. 617, 629 (1978).

4. Ibid., 632.

5. Ibid., 624, citing *Pike v. Bruce Church, Inc.,* 397 U.S. 137 (1970). See also Murray and Spence, "Fair Weather Federalism," 77.

6. *Chemical Waste Management, Inc. v. Hunt,* 504 U.S. 332 (1992); *Fort Gratiot Sanitary Landfill, Inc. v. Michigan Department of Natural Resources,* 504 U.S. 332 (1992); *Oregon Waste Systems, Inc. v. Department of Environmental Quality of Oregon,* 511 U.S. 93 (1994); Murray and Spence, "Fair Weather Federalism."

7. Murray and Spence, "Fair Weather Federalism"; Verchick, "Commerce Clause."

8. Michael Diederich, "Should Municipalities or Businesses Control Trash Handling?" letter to the editor, *New York Times,* December 7, 1993.

9. Murray and Spence, "Fair Weather Federalism"; Adler, "Stopping the Garbage Monopoly."

10. Virginia Department of Environmental Quality, "Solid Waste Managed in Virginia, 2007."

11. PBS News Hour online, "Trash Trouble," January 28, 1999, http://www.pbs .org/newshour/bb/environment/jan-june99/trash_1-28.html; John Tierney, "The Big City; A Fair Place to Find Peace; Trash for Vice," *New York Times,* January 25, 1999.

12. The bills in question are SB865ER, passed by the General Assembly on March 12, 1999; the governor's substitute was CHAP097, adopted by the General Assembly on April 7, 1999. The legislative sequence of events is tracked online at http://leg1.state.va.us/cgi-bin/legp504.exe?991+sum+SB865. Information on

Treacy's background and contributions to Gilmore from the waste management industry are documented in Lipton, "Gilmore Orders Moratorium on Construction."

13. *Waste Management Holdings v. Gilmore*, 252 F.3d 316 (4th Cir. 2001); Michael D. Shear, "Warner Tried to 'Govern from the Center,' " *Washington Post,* April 7, 2005. According to Karen Sismour, director of the Virginia Department of Environmental Quality's Waste Division, none of the following bills, calling for modest per-ton fees on MSW, passed the Virginia General Assembly: "In 2002, Governor Warner proposed an amendment to SB592 to: impose a $5 per ton state fee on all solid waste landfilled in Virginia and use the funds to provide grants to localities, to support the Virginia Land Conservation Fund, to improve water quality, for remediation and restoration of brownfield sites and to support DEQ's program costs. In 2004, HB 1462 was introduced to establish a $5 per ton fee on municipal solid waste to be collected by localities in which the landfills are located. The host localities would retain 50% for the abatement of pollution caused by landfills or the improper management of waste, groundwater monitoring and cleanup, litter control, recycling, or for other waste-related purposes, including solid waste management operating fees. The host localities would remit 50% of all moneys collected to the Commonwealth to be deposited into the Landfill Cleanup and Closure Fund, the Virginia Brownfields Restoration and Economic Redevelopment Assistance Fund, and the Virginia Environmental Emergency Response Fund. This bill was continued to 2005. In 2005, HB1760 was introduced to establish a $1 per ton surcharge on all solid waste disposed of in sanitary landfills; however this bill never made it out of committee. It is estimated that the bill would have generated approximately $13.9 M annually. $6.95 M (50%) would have been retained by localities and the other $6.95 M would have been deposited to the Virginia Solid Waste Management and Clean-up Fund (this fund would have been created if the bill had passed) and the Water Quality Improvement Fund. In 2007, HB1945 was introduced, to require landfill owners or operators pay a fee ranging from $0.50 to $1.00 for each ton of solid waste received at the landfill. The fee would increase commensurate with the volume of solid waste disposed of at the landfill. Moneys would be deposited into the general fund. The bill did not pass." Sismour to author, February 26, 2008.

14. *USA Recycling, Inc. v. Town of Babylon*, 66 F.3d 1272, 1295 (2d Circuit 1995).

15. *United Haulers Association v. Oneida-Herkimer Solid Waste Management Authority,* 127 S.Ct. 1786, 1795 (U.S., April 30, 2007).

16. Ibid.

17. *Paul's Industrial Garage v. City of Red Wing,* 2006 U.S. Dist., LEXIS 92960; *National Solid Waste Management Association v. Daviess County, Kentucky,* 446 F.3d 647 (6th Cir. 2006); National Solid Wastes Management Association, "Flow Control of Solid Wastes," http://wastec.isproductions.net/webmodules/webarticles/anmviewer.asp?a=1085.

18. CBC News, "Michigan Dumps Toronto Garbage"; City of Toronto, "Facts about Toronto's Trash."

19. Sussex and Charles City counties, *amicus curiae* brief, *United Haulers Associa-*

tion v. Oneida-Herkimer Solid Waste Management Authority, 438 F.3d 150 (2d Cir. 2006), cert. granted.

20. Murray and Spence, "Fair Weather Federalism," supplemented by an online search using the Library of Congress's online search engine, "Thomas," August 28, 2008.

21. Voinovich introduced the *Solid Waste Interstate Transportation and Local Authority Act of 1999*, S 663, 106th Cong., 1st sess., http://thomas.loc.gov/cgi-bin/bdquery/z?d106:SN00663:@@@D&summ2=m&. Minge's bill was the *Taxpayer Relief through Municipal Waste Control Act of 1999*, HR 1270, 106th Cong., 1st sess., http://thomas.loc.gov/cgi-bin/bdquery/z?d106:HR01270:@@@D&summ2=m&.

22. U.S. Senate Committee on Environment and Public Works, *Transportation and Flow Control of Solid Waste*, 17; New Jersey Department of Environmental Protection, *State Wide Solid Waste Management Plan 2006*, executive summary, http://www.state.nj.us/dep/dshw/recycling/swmp/pdf/execsumm06.pdf.

23. Randy Johnson, Chair, Hennepin, Minnesota, County Board of Supervisors, John Skinner, President, SWANA, testimony before U.S. Senate Committee on Environment and Public Works, *Transportation and Flow Control of Solid Waste*.

24. National Association of Counties, "Supreme Court to Hear Garbage Case." To my knowledge, the National Association of Counties does not name the counties that have suffered these "countless problems." In response to my e-mail inquiry on this point, Julie Ufner of NACo responded that she had no specific examples on record and referred me to a contact in an Ohio solid waste agency. Julie Ufner to author, January 16, 2007.

25. *United Haulers v. Oneida-Herkimer Solid Waste*, respondent brief at pp. 3–4, 127 S.Ct. 1786 (U.S., April 30, 2007).

26. Testimony of Senator Bob Smith, U.S. Senate Committee on Environment and Public Works, *Interstate Waste and Flow Control*, 163.

27. *Municipal Solid Waste Interstate Transportation and Local Authority Act of 2003*, S 431, 108th Cong., 1st sess., *Congressional Record* 149 (Feb. 24, 2003): S 2594.

28. *International Solid Waste Importation and Management Act of 2006*, HR 2491, 109th Cong., 2d sess., http://thomas.loc.gov/cgi-bin/bdquery/z?d109:HR02491:@@@L&summ2=m&.

29. *State Waste Empowerment and Enforcement Provision Act of 2007*, HR 70, 110th Cong., 1st sess., http://thomas.loc.gov/cgi-bin/bdquery/D?d110:1:./temp/07Ebda6Z4:@@@L&summ2=m&|/bss/110search.html|; *Solid Waste Interstate Transportation Act of 2007*, HR 274, 110th Cong., 1st sess., http://thomas.loc.gov/cgi-bin/bdquery/D?d110:1:./temp/7Ebd5TQ3:@@@L&summ2=m&|/bss/110search.html|.

30. *Municipal Solid Waste Interstate Transportation and Local Authority Act of 2003*, S 431, 108th Cong., 1st sess., *Congressional Record* 149 (Feb. 24, 2003): S 2594.

31. *Solid Waste Interstate Transportation and Local Authority Act of 1999*, S 663, 106th Cong., 1st sess., http://thomas.loc.gov/cgi-bin/bdquery/z?d106:SN00663:@@@D&summ2=m&.

32. Bruce Parker, National Solid Waste Management Association, testimony be-

fore U.S. Senate Committee on Environment and Public Works, *Interstate Waste and Flow Control*, 49.

33. National Education Association, *Rankings and Estimates*, tables F-10 and F-13.

34. Burnley, "Statement of Robert K. Burnley"; U.S. Environmental Protection Agency, "Kim-Stan Landfill."

35. Burnley, "Statement of Robert K. Burnley," 35 (emphasis added).

36. Environmental Law Institute, *Greening the Budget 2005*.

37. U.S. Government Accountability Office, "Superfund."

5. Solving the Genuine Problems of Long-Distance Trash Transport

1. Felicity Barringer, "A City Committed to Recycling Is Ready for More," *New York Times*, May 7, 2008; Trymaine Lee, "A Crackdown on Recycling Spurs Some Vigilance," *New York Times*, January 1, 2008; Niblack, "Cost Comparison"; New York City Department of City Planning, *Final Comprehensive Solid Waste Management Plan*, 2–8; Hess, "Out-of-State, Out of Mind," testimony before the Senate Committee on Environment and Public Works, *Interstate Waste and Flow Control*.

2. Virginia Department of Environmental Quality, "Solid Waste Managed in Virginia, 2007."

3. Lipton, "As Imported Garbage Piles Up, So Do Worries"; Lipton, "Crackdown on Trucks Leaves Piles of Trash"; Taylor, "Talking Trash."

4. "Wisconsin Waste Haulers Work with EPA to Cut Diesel Emissions," *Waste-Age*, January 19, 2007, http://wasteage.com/news/EPA_MCDI/; Virginia Department of Environmental Quality, "Solid Waste Managed in Virginia, 2007"; Pennsylvania DEP, "Municipal and Residual Waste Transportation."

5. Price, "Landfill Directive"; Canterbury and Eisenfeld, "Rise of Pay-as-You-Throw."

6. U.S. Environmental Protection Agency, "MSW Programs" and "Municipal Solid Waste, 2007."

7. "Seattle Makes Recycling Mandatory," *Recycling Today*, February 2004, 8.

8. Strasser, *Waste and Want*.

9. District of Columbia, *Public Report on Recycling, 2005–2007*.

10. California Integrated Waste Management Board, *Curbside Recycling, the Next Generation;* Rebecca Kaufman, "New Hampshire Towns Are Talking Trash," New Hampshire Public Radio, February 22, 2006, *http://www.nhpr.org/node/10338*.

11. Canterbury and Eisenfeld, "Rise of Pay-as-You-Throw"; San Francisco Commission on the Environment, "Resolution Adopting a Date of 2020"; Gunther, "Wal-Mart Trashes Garbage"; Carolyn Jones, "Powered by Pooches: Rather than Let Pet Dung Go to Waste, Experts Explore Its Energy Potential," *San Francisco Chronicle*, February 21, 2006.

12. Quoted in Jane Gordon, "The Right to Bear Trash," *New York Times*, August 31, 2003.

13. Wal-Mart Stores, "Zero Waste," http://www.walmartstores.com/sustainability/7762.aspx; Gunther, "Wal-Mart Trashes Garbage"; Xerox Corporation, *Revealing True Colors;* Fetzer Vineyards, "Fetzer's Environmental Commitment," *http://www.fetzer.com/assets/wineries/fetz_envi.pdf*; Epson Portland, "2008 Green Permit Annual Report"; Weeks, "Take This Product Back."

14. Sheehan and Spiegelman, "Extended Producer Responsibility"; New York City, "Wastele$$ Business," http://www.nyc.gov/html/nycwasteless/html/in_business/product_stewardship.shtml; INFORM, *California's and Maine's Electronics Recycling Programs*.

15. Sheehan and Spiegelman, "Extended Producer Responsibility"; Lynch, " 'Extended' Producer Responsibility."

16. Sachs, "Planning the Funeral at Birth"; European Commission, "Waste."

17. Sachs, "Planning the Funeral at Birth."

18. Ibid.

19. Ackerman, *Why Do We Recycle?*; U.S. Environmental Protection Agency, "Recycling Is Working."

20. Williams and Matheny, *Democracy, Dialogue, and Environmental Disputes*.

21. U.S. Environmental Protection Agency, "Closure and Post-Closure Requirements."

22. Lipton, "Friends Help Industry Protect Itself"; Commonwealth of Pennsylvania, "Rendell Enacts Growing Greener II"; Pennsylvania DEP, "Amount of Waste Deposited in PA Landfills"; U.S. Congressional Research Service, *Interstate Shipment of MSW: 2007 Update*; Paula Wolf, "New State Trash Tax Won't Affect Consumers," *Lancaster (PA) Sunday News*, September 15, 2002.

23. Shean, "Politics of Trash."

24. Okuda and Thomson, "Regionalization in Japan"; Yoshida "Case Studies in Japan."

25. Repa, "NSWMA's 2005 Tip Fee Survey"; Okuda and Thomson, "Regionalization."

26. Adler, "Stopping the Garbage Monopoly."

Bibliography

Ackerman, Frank. *Why Do We Recycle?* Washington, D.C.: Island Press, 1997.

Adler, Jonathan H. "Judicial Federalism and the Future of Federal Environmental Regulation." *Iowa Law Review* 90, no. 1 (2005): 377–474.

———. "Stopping the Garbage Monopoly." *Journal of Commerce*, September 2, 1994.

Andrews, J. Douglas. "Landfills: Host Fees Helps [*sic*] Create Landfill Capacity in Illinois." *Waste Age*, November 1, 1996. *http://wasteage.com/mag/waste_land fills_host_fees/index.html*.

Angotti, Tom. "City's New Waste Plan and the Neighborhoods." *Gotham (New York) Gazette*, July 2006. *http://www.gothamgazette.com/article/landuse/ 20060725/12/1921*.

Associated Press. "Towering Piles of Trash Threaten to Engulf Europe." *St. Louis Post Dispatch*, January 6, 1995.

Astrup, T., G. Cappai, O. Hjelmer, A. Kihl, P. Lechner, P. Mostbauer, M. Nyholm, A. Polettnini, R. Pomi, H. A. van der Sloot, A. van Zomeren. "Towards an Improved Understanding of the Leaching Behavior of MSWI Residues—Report on the 2nd Meeting of the IWWG Phoenix Working Group on 'Management of Municipal Solid Waste Incineration Residues.' " *Waste Management* 24 (2004): 529–30.

Baldwin, Richard. "Does Sustainability Require Growth?" In *The Economics of Sustainable Development*, ed. Ian Goldin and L. Alan Winters. Cambridge: Cambridge University Press, 1995.

Barber, Benjamin. *Con$umed: How Markets Corrupt Children, Infantilize Adults, and Swallow Citizens Whole*. New York: W. W. Norton, 2007.

Beckerman, Wilfred. *Small Is Stupid: Blowing the Whistle on the Greens*. London: Duckworth, 1995.

Been, Vicki. "Locally Undesirable Land Uses in Minority Neighborhoods: Disproportionate Siting or Market Dynamics?" *Yale Law Journal* 103, no. 6 (1994): 1383–1422.

Bullard, Robert D. *Dumping in Dixie: Race, Class, and Environmental Quality*. Boulder, Colo.: Westview Press, 2000.

———. "Environmental Justice in the 21st Century." In *Debating the Earth: The Environmental Politics Reader*, ed. John Dryzek, 429–31. Oxford: Oxford University Press, 2005.

Bullard, Robert D., and Beverly Hendrix Wright. "The Politics of Pollution: Implications for the Black Community." *Phylon* 47, no. 1 (1986): 71–78.

Burnley, Robert. "Statement of Robert K. Burnley, Director, Virginia Department of Environmental Quality, Before the Senate Committee on Environment and Public Works." *Interstate Waste and Flow Control: Hearing before the Senate Committee on Environment and Public Works.* 107th Cong., 2d sess., March 20, 2002. *http://epw.senate.gov/107th/Burnley_032002.htm.*

Burnley, Stephen. "The Impact of the European Landfill Directive on Waste Management in the United Kingdom." *Resources, Conservation, and Recycling* 32 (2001): 349–58.

California Integrated Waste Management Board. *Summary: "Innovations" Case Studies; Curbside Recycling, the Next Generation.* Sacramento, Calif.: California Integrated Waste Management Board, 2007. http://www.ciwmb.ca.gov/lglibrary/Innovations/Curbside/Summary.htm.

Canterbury, Janice, and Sue Eisenfeld. "The Rise . . . and Rise of Pay-as-You-Throw." *MSW Management,* n.d. http://www.mswmanagement.com/elements-2006/waste-management-challenges-2.aspx.

Canterbury, Janice, and Ryan Newill. "The Pay-As-You-Throw Payoff." *American City and County,* October 1, 2003. http://www.americancityandcounty.com/mag/government_payasyouthrow_payoff/.

CBC News. "Michigan Dumps Toronto Garbage by 2010," August 31, 2006. http://www.cbc.ca/canada/toronto/story/2006/08/31/trash-michigan.html#skip300x250.

Christenson, Scott C., and Isabelle M. Cozzarelli. *The Norman Landfill Environmental Research Site: What Happens to Waste in Landfills?* Washington, D.C.: U.S. Geological Survey, 2003. *http://pubs.usgs.gov/fs/fs-040-03/#protection1988.*

Colten, Craig E. "Chicago's Waste Lands: Refuse Disposal and Urban Growth, 1840–1990." *Journal of Historical Geography* 20, no. 2 (1994): 124–42.

Crenson, Matthew. *The Un-politics of Air Pollution: A Study of Non-Decisionmaking in the Cities.* Baltimore: Johns Hopkins Press, 1971.

Daly, Herman. *Beyond Growth: The Economics of Sustainable Development.* Boston: Beacon Press, 1994.

Davis, Devra. *When Smoke Ran Like Water: Tales of Environmental Deception and the Battle against Pollution.* New York: Basic Books, 2002.

Diamond, Jared. *Collapse: How Societies Choose to Fail or Succeed.* New York: Viking, 2005.

District of Columbia. *Public Report on Recycling: Fiscal Years 2005–2007.* Washington, D.C.: Government of the District of Columbia, 2008. http://dc.gov/mayor/pdf/showpdf.asp?pdfname=FY05-07.pdf.

Duffy, Daniel P. "Landfill Economics Part II: Getting Down to Business." *MSW Management,* July–August 2005. *http://www.mswmanagement.com/mw_0507_landfill2.html.*

———. "Landfill Macroeconomics: Taking the Big Picture." *MSW Management,*

November–December 2006. http://www.forester.net/mw_0611_macroec onomics.html.

Ehrlich, Paul R., and Anne H. Ehrlich. "The Population Explosion: Why We Should Care and What We Should Do About It." *Environmental Law* 27, no. 4 (1997): 1187–1208.

Eklund, Bart, Eric P. Anderson, Barry L. Walker, and Don B. Burrows. "Characterization of Landfill Gas Composition at the Fresh Kills Municipal Solid Waste Landfill." *Environmental Science and Technology* 32, no. 15 (1998): 2233–37.

El-Fadel, Mutasim, Angelos N. Findikakis, and James O. Leckie. "Environmental Impacts of Solid Waste Landfilling." *Journal of Environmental Management* 50 (1997): 1–25.

Environmental Law Institute. *Greening the Budget 2005: 6 Ways to Save Taxpayer Dollars and Protect the Environment in the Commonwealth of Virginia.* Washington, D.C.: Environmental Law Institute, October 2004.

Epson Portland, Inc. "2008 Green Permit Annual Report." Hillsboro, Ore.: Epson Portland, Inc., 2008. http://www.epi.epson.com/env/fy08_green_permit_ annual_report.pdf.

Ernst, Natasha. "Flow Control Ordinances in a Post-*Carbone* World." *Penn State Environmental Law Review* 13 (2004): 53–84.

European Commission. "Biodegradable Waste." Brussels: European Commission, 2007. http://ec.europa.eu/environment/waste/compost/index.htm.

———. *EU Focus on Waste Management.* Luxembourg: European Communities, 1999.

———. *Europe in Figures: Eurostat Yearbook, 2006–7.* Luxembourg: Eurostat, 2007. http://epp.eurostat.ec.europa.eu/portal/page?_pageid=1073,46587259&_ dad=portal&_schema=PORTAL&p_product_code=KS-CD-06-001.

———. "Waste." Brussels: European Commission, 2007. *http://ec.europa.eu/environ ment/waste/index.htm.*

———. *Waste Generated and Treated in Europe, 1990–2001.* Luxembourg: European Commission, 2003.

———. *Waste Prevention and Minimisation: Final Report.* Brussels: European Commission, 1999. http:// ec.europa.eu/environment/waste/studies/pdf/prevention_minimisation.pdf.

European Environment Agency. "Addressing the Economics of Waste." Copenhagen: EEA, 2004. *http://213.253.134.29/oecd/pdfs/browseit/ 9704031E.PDF.*

———. "Country Fact Sheets on Waste Management." Copenhagen: European Topic Centre on Resource and Waste Management, 2007. http://waste.eionet.europa .eu/facts/factsheets_waste.

———. *Effectiveness of Packaging Waste Management Systems in Selected Countries: An EEA Pilot Study.* Copenhagen: EEA, 2005. http://reports.eea.europa.eu/eea_ report_2005_3/en/FINAL-3_05-Packaging_waste_WEB.pdf.

———. *Environmental Outlook: Municipal Waste.* Copenhagen: EEA, 2007. http:// waste.eionet.europa.eu/wp/wp/_2007.

———. *Environment in the European Union at the Turn of the Century.* Copenhagen: EEA, 1999. http://reports.eea.europa.eu/92-9157-202-0/en/page307.html.

————. *Europe's Environment: The Fourth Assessment.* Copenhagen: EEA, 2007. http://reports.eea.europa.eu/state_of_environment_report_2007_/en.

————. *Europe's Environment: The Third Assessment.* Chapter 7, "Waste." Copenhagen: EEA, 2003. http://reports.eea.eu.int/environmental_assessment_report_2003_10/Chapter7.

————. *Household and Municipal Waste: Comparability of Data in EEA Member Countries.* Copenhagen: EEA, 2000. http://reports.eea.eu.int/Topic_report_No_32000/en.

————. *Household Consumption and the Environment.* Copenhagen: EEA, 2005. http://reports.eea.europa.eu/eea_report_2005_11/en/EEA_report_11_2005.pdf.

————. "Municipal Waste Generated Per Capita, 1995–2005." Luxembourg: European Communities, 2007. http://dataservice.eea.europa.eu/atlas/viewdata/viewpub.asp?id=1739.

————. "Municipal Waste Generation—Assessment Published January 2008." Copenhagen: EEA. http://themes.eea.europa.eu/IMS/ISpecs/ISpecification 20041007131809/IAssessment1183020255530/view_content.

————. *Waste: Annual Topic Update 1998.* Copenhagen: EEA, 1999. http://reports .eea.europa.eu/92-9167-140-1/en/topic_6_1999.pdf.

European Environment Bureau. "The Quality of National Implementation of the Landfill Directive." Brussels: European Environment Bureau, 2005. http:// www.eeb.org/activities/waste/landfill/snapshot-report-landfill-directive-August2005.pdf.

European Union. "Packaging and Packaging Waste." European Parliament and Council Directive 94/62/EC of December 20, 1994. Brussels: EU, 2007. http:// europa.eu/scadplus/leg/en/lvb/l21207.htm.

Faber, Daniel R., and Eric J. Krieg. "Unequal Exposure to Ecological Hazards: Environmental Injustices in the Commonwealth of Massachusetts." *Environmental Health Perspectives* 110 (2002): 277–88.

Foreman, Christopher H. *The Promise and Peril of Environmental Justice.* Washington, D.C.: Brookings Institution, 1998.

Goldstein, Nora. "The State of Garbage in America." *Biocycle* 41, no. 4 (2000): 32–39.

Griffin, Rodman D. "Garbage Crisis." *CQ Researcher,* March 20, 1992. http:// library.cqpress.com/cqres/.

Grossman, Gene M. "Pollution and Growth: What Do We Know?" In *The Economics of Sustainable Development,* ed. Ian Goldin and L. Alan Winters. A publication of the OECD and the Centre for Economic Policy Research. Cambridge: Cambridge University Press, 1995.

Grossman, Gene M., and Alan B. Krueger. "Economic Growth and the Environment." *Quarterly Journal of Economics,* 110, no. 2 (1995): 353–77.

Gunther, Marc. "Wal-Mart Trashes Garbage." *Fortune,* January 11, 2007. http://money .cnn.com/2007/01/10/magazines/fortune/zerowaste.fortune/index.htm.

Harper, Scott. "Import of Out-of-State Waste Rises Sharply for Virginia." *Virginian Pilot,* June 16, 2005.

Harvey, Ross. "Comparison of Household Saving Ratios: Euro Area/United States/Japan." *OECD Statistics Brief* no. 8 (June 2004): 1–8. http://www.oecd .org/dataoecd/53/48/32023442.pdf.

Hird, John A. *Superfund: The Political Economy of Environmental Risk.* Baltimore: Johns Hopkins University Press, 1994.

Hurley, Andrew. *Environmental Inequalities: Class, Race, and Industrial Pollution in Gary, Indiana, 1945–1980.* Chapel Hill: University of North Carolina Press, 1995.

Hussen, Ahmed M. *Principles of Environmental Economics: Economics, Ecology, and Public Policy.* London: Routledge, 2000.

INFORM. *A Review of California's and Maine's Electronics Recycling Programs.* New York: INFORM, February 2007.

Institute for Applied Ecology. *Waste Prevention and Minimisation: Final Report.* Commissioned by the European Commission. Darmstadt: IAE, July 29, 1999. http:// ec.europa.eu/environment/waste/studies/pdf/prevention_minimisation.pdf.

Integrated Waste Services Association. "Fact Sheet: Waste-to-Energy Ash Residue." http://www.wte.org/docs/FactSheetAsh.pdf.

Kahn, Joseph, and Mark Landler, "China Grabs West's Smoke-Spewing Factories," *New York Times,* December 21, 2007.

Kahn, Joseph, and Jim Yardley. "As China Roars, Pollution Reaches Deadly Extremes." *New York Times,* August 26, 2007.

Kaufman, Scott M., Nora Goldstein, Karsten Millrath, and Nickolas J. Themelis. "The State of Garbage in America." *BioCycle* 45, no. 1 (2004): 31–41. http://www .jgpress.com/archives/_free/000089.html#more.

Kiger, Patrick. "Living Ever Larger: How Wretched Excess Became a Way of Life in Southern California." *Los Angeles Times Magazine,* June 9, 2002.

King County, Washington, Solid Waste Division. "2006 Solid Waste Division Annual Report." King County, Wash.: Dept. of Natural Resources and Parks, 2007. http://www.metrokc.gov/dnrp/swd/about/documents/SWD_annual_ report-2006.pdf.

Knickerbocker, Brad. "Katrina Lays Bare Superfund Woes." *Christian Science Monitor,* September 15, 2005. http://www.csmonitor.com/2005/0915/p02s01-sten .html.

Lipton, Eric. "As Imported Garbage Piles Up, So Do Worries; 3 Million Tons of Trash Enter Virginia Each Year." *Washington Post,* November 12, 1998.

———. "City Trash Follows Long and Winding Road." *New York Times,* March 24, 1999.

———. "Crackdown on Trucks Leaves Piles of Trash in New York." *New York Times,* June 16, 1999.

———. "Friends Help Industry Protect Itself." *Washington Post,* November 14, 1998.

———. "Gilmore Orders Moratorium on Construction, Expansion of Landfills." *Washington Post,* November 14, 1998.

Louis, Garrick. "A Historical Context of Municipal Solid Waste Management in the United States." *Waste Management and Research* 22 (August 2004): 306–22.

Lynch, Allen. " 'Extended' Producer Responsibility—Why Not?" *MSW Management*, January–February 2007.

Mazzanti, Massimiliano, Anna Montini, and Roberto Zoboli. "Municipal Waste Generation and Socioeconomic Drivers: Evidence from Comparing Northern and Southern Italy." *Journal of the Environment and Development* 17, no. 1 (2008): 51–69.

McDonough, William, and Michael Braungart. *Cradle to Cradle: Remaking the Way We Make Things*. New York: North Point Press, 2002.

McGovern, Dan. *The Campo Indian Landfill War: The Fight for Gold in California's Garbage*. Norman: University of Oklahoma Press, 1995.

Melosi, Martin V. *Garbage in the Cities: Refuse, Reform, and the Environment, 1880–1980*. Pittsburgh: University of Pittsburgh Press, 2005.

Merrill, Thomas C. "Golden Rules for Transboundary Pollution." *Duke Law Journal* 46 (March 1997): 931–1019.

Miller, Benjamin. *Fat of the Land: Garbage in New York, the Last Two Hundred Years*. New York: Four Walls Eight Windows, 2000.

Miller, Chaz. "Losing Count: Can We Track the True Size of the US Waste Stream?" *Waste Age*, November 1, 2007. http://wasteage.com/Waste_Legislation/waste_losing_count/index.html.

Montgomery, David R. "Effects of the Loma Prieta Earthquake, October 17, 1989, San Francisco Bay Area." *California Geology* 43, no. 1 (1990). http://www.johnmartin.com/earthquake/eqpapers/00000080.htm.

Mooallem, Jon. "The Afterlife of Cell Phones." *New York Times*, January 13, 2008.

Murray, Paula C., and David B. Spence. "Fair Weather Federalism and America's Waste Disposal Crisis." *Harvard Environmental Law Review* 27 (2003): 71–103.

National Education Association. *Rankings and Estimates: Rankings of the States 2006 and Estimates of School Statistics 2007*. Atlanta: NEA Research, 2007. *http://www.nea.org/edstats/images/07rankings.pdf*.

National Environmental Justice Advisory Council. *A Regulatory Strategy for Siting and Operating Waste Transfer Stations*. Washington, D.C.: EPA, 2000.

New Jersey, State of. *State Wide Solid Waste Management Plan 2006*. Trenton: New Jersey Department of Environmental Protection, December 28, 2005. *http://www.state.nj.us/dep/dshw/recycle/swmp/index.html*.

New York City Department of City Planning. "Fresh Kills Park Project." New York: City of New York, 2006. http://www.nyc.gov/html/dcp/html/fkl/fkl3.shtml.

New York City Department of Sanitation. *Comprehensive Solid Waste Management Plan*. New York: Department of Sanitation, 2006. http://www.nyc.gov/html/dsny/html/swmp/swmp-4oct.shtml.

———. "Request for Expressions of Interest to Provide Waste Disposal Capacity." New York: Department of Sanitation, 2004. http://concernedcitizens.homestead.com/files/NYC/BLOOMBERG_REQUEST_FOR_EXPRESSION_INTEREST_NYC_WASTE.pdf.

New York State Department of Environmental Conservation. "Solid Waste Management Facilities." Albany, N.Y.: DEC, 2008. http://www.dec.ny.gov/chemical/8495.html.

Niblack, Preston. "Cost Comparison: The New York City Independent Budget Office Says More Recycling Could Help to Lower the City's Trash Costs." *Recycling Today*, July 2007. http://findarticles.com/p/articles/mi_moKWH/is_7_45/ai_n19394686/pg_1.

Nosenchuck, Norman H. "The 25th Anniversary of the New York State Department of Environmental Conservation: Past and Future Challenges and Directions; Key Events of the New York State Solid Waste Management Program, 1970–1995." *Albany Law Journal of Science and Technology* 7 (1996): 69–96.

Okuda, Itaru. "State of Waste Management in Japan." Unpublished paper, 2005.

Okuda, Itaru, and Vivian E. Thomson. "Regionalization of Municipal Solid Waste Management in Japan: Roles of the Proximity Principle, Central Government Control, and Local Government Financing." *Environmental Management* 40 (2007): 12–19.

Onishi, Norimitsu. "How Do Japanese Dump Trash? Let Us Count the Myriad Ways." *New York Times*, May 12, 2005.

Onorato, Danielle. "Japanese Recycling Law Takes Effect." *Waste Age*, June 1, 2001. http://wasteage.com/mag/waste_japanese_recycling_law/.

Organisation for Economic Cooperation and Development. "OECD Factbook 2007: Economic, Environmental, and Social Statistics." http://masetto.sourceoecd.org/vl=1165386/cl=12/nw=1/npsu/fact2007/.

———. "OECD Factbook 2007: Household Saving." http://masetto.sourceoecd.org/vl=1165386/cl=12/nw=1/npsu/fact2007/.

———. "Population Statistics for OECD Countries, 1988 through 2003." July 15, 2005. http://masetto.sourceoecd.org/vl=1165386/cl=12/nw=1/npsu/fact2007/.

Packard, Vance Oakley. *The Waste Makers*. New York: D. McKay, 1960.

Park, Jill. "Casemakers Converted to the Lighter Side." *Packaging News*, March 11, 2008. http://www.packagingnews.co.uk/news/789643/Casemakers-converted-lighter-side/.

Pellow, David Naguib. *Garbage Wars: The Struggle for Environmental Justice in Chicago*. Cambridge: MIT Press, 2002.

Pennsylvania, Commonwealth of. "Governor Rendell Enacts Growing Greener II, Makes Historic Investment in Environment, Economy." Press Release, July 2005. *http://www.state.pa.us/papower/cwp/view.asp?A=11&Q=444209*.

Pennsylvania Department of Environmental Protection. "Amount of Waste Deposited in PA Landfills Down for Fourth Consecutive Year." Harrisburg: Pennsylvania DEP, 2006. *http://www.depweb.state.pa.us/news/cwp/view.asp?a=3&q=504640*.

———. "Municipal and Residual Waste Transportation and Safety Program." Harrisburg: Pennsylvania DEP, 2002. http://www.depweb.state.pa.us/landrecwaste/cwp/view.asp?a=1238&Q=463529&landrecwasteNav=|.

Pierog, Karen. "Two Ohio Waste Incinerators Close, Partly Due to May High Court Ruling." *Bond Buyer*, November 9, 1994.

Piggin, Jean-Baptiste. "Germany Importing Extra Rubbish." *Independent Online*, April 13, 2004. *http://www.iol.co.za/index.php?click_id=143&art_id=qw1081883340970B265&set_id=1*.

Price, Janet. "The Landfill Directive and the Challenge Ahead: Demands and Pressures on the UK Householder." *Resources, Conservation, and Recycling* 32, nos. 3–4 (2001): 333–48.

Prystay, Cris. "Recycling—Gadget Regurgitator." *Far Eastern Economic Review,* September 30, 2004, 42.

Puder, Marcus. "Trash, Ash, and the Phoenix: A Fifth Anniversary Review of the Supreme Court's City of Chicago Waste-To-Energy Combustion Ash Decision." *Boston College Environmental Affairs Law Review* 26 (1999): 473–517.

Pulido, Laura. *Environmentalism and Economic Justice: Two Chicano Struggles in the Southwest.* Tucson: University of Arizona Press, 1996.

———. "Rethinking Environmental Racism: White Privilege and Urban Development in Southern California." *Annals of the Association of American Geographers* 90, no. 1 (2000): 12–40.

Rathje, William, and Cullen Murphy. *Rubbish! The Archaeology of Garbage.* New York: Harper Collins, 2001.

Repa, Edward W. "Interstate Movement of Solid Waste—1995 Update." *Waste Age* 28, no. 6 (1997): 40–57.

———. "NSWMA's 2005 Tip Fee Survey." NSWMA Research Bulletin 05-3, March 2005. http://wastec.isproductions.net/webmodules/webarticles/articlefiles/478-Tipping%20Fee%20Bulletin%202005.pdf.

———. "Solid Waste Disposal Trends." *Waste Age,* April 1, 2000. http://wasteage.com/mag/waste_solid_waste_disposal/index.html.

Rhodes, Edwardo Lao. *Environmental Justice in America: A New Paradigm.* Bloomington: Indiana University Press, 2003.

Ringquist, Evan. "A Question of Justice: Equity in Environmental Litigation, 1974–1991." *Journal of Politics* 60, no. 4 (1998): 1148–65.

Rothman, Dale S. "Environmental Kuznets Curve: Real Progress or Passing the Buck? A Case for Consumption-Based Approaches." *Ecological Economics* 25, no. 2 (1998): 177–94.

Rothman, Dale S., and Sander M. de Bruyn. "Probing into the Environmental Kuznets Curve Hypothesis." *Ecological Economics* 25, no. 2 (1998): 143–45.

Royte, Elizabeth. "E-gad! Americans Discard More than 100 Million Computers, Cell Phones and Other Electronic Devices Each Year." *Smithsonian,* August 2005. http://www.smithsonianmag.com/arts-culture/e-gad.html.

———. *Garbage Land: On the Secret Trail of Trash.* New York: Little, Brown, 2005.

Sabbas, T., et al. "Management of Municipal Solid Waste Incineration Residues." *Waste Management* 23, no. 1 (2003): 61–88.

Sachs, Noah. "Planning the Funeral at Birth: Extended Producer Responsibility in the European Union and the United States." *Harvard Environmental Law Review* 30 (2006): 51–98.

San Francisco Commission on the Environment. "Resolution Adopting a Date of 2020 for San Francisco to Achieve the Goal of Zero Waste to Landfill and Directing the Department of the Environment to Develop Policies and Programs to Increase Producer and Consumer Responsibility in Order to Achieve the Zero

Waste Goal." San Francisco: San Francisco Department of the Environment, 2006. *http://www.sfgov.org/site/sfenvironment_page.asp?id=15792*.

San Francisco Department of Solid Waste. "Building a Bright Future: San Francisco's Environmental Plan 2008." http://www.sfgov.org/site/uploadedfiles/mayor/SForwardFinal.pdf.

Schor, Juliet. *The Overspent American: Upscaling, Downshifting, and the New Consumer.* New York: Basic Books, 1998.

Schumacher, E. F. *Small Is Beautiful: Economics as If People Mattered.* New York: Harper & Row, 1973.

Schwartz, Martin A. "The Commerce Clause Quartet." *New York Law Journal* (October 18, 1994).

Schwerin, Jennifer, and Leslie Schwerin. *Talking Trash.* VHS. New York: First Run/Icarus Films, 1994.

Selden, Thomas M., Anne S. Forrest, and James E. Lockhart. "Analyzing the Reductions in U.S. Air Pollution Emissions: 1970 to 1990." *Land Economics* 75 (February 1999): 1–21.

Shafik, Nemat. "Economic Development and Environmental Quality: An Econometric Analysis." *Oxford Economic Papers* 46 (1994): 757–73.

Shams, Rasul. "Dollar-Euro Exchange Rate, 1999–2004—Dollar and Euro as International Currencies." Hamburg Welt-Wirtschafts-Archiv Discussion Paper, 2005. http://www.hwwa.de/Forschung/Publikationen/Discussion_Paper/2005/321.pdf.

Shean, Daniel. "The Politics of Trash." Working paper, University of Virginia Law School, 2008.

Sheehan, Bill, and Helen Spiegelman. "Extended Producer Responsibility Policies in the United States and Canada." In *Governance of Integrated Product Policy: In Search of Sustainable Production and Consumption,* ed. Dirk Scheer and Frieder Rubik. Sheffield, UK: Greenleaf, 2005. http://www.productpolicy.org/assets/pdf/EPR_in_USA_Canada_Ch14.pdf.

Shrader-Frechette, K. S. *Burying Uncertainty: The Case against Geological Disposal of High-Level Nuclear Waste.* Berkeley and Los Angeles: University of California Press, 1993.

———. *Environmental Justice: Creating Equality, Reclaiming Democracy.* Oxford: Oxford University Press, 2005.

Simmons, Phil, Nora Goldstein, Scott M. Kaufman, Nicolas J. Themelis, and James Thompson Jr. "The State of Garbage in America." *BioCycle* 47, no. 4 (2006): 26–43. http://www.jgpress.com/archives/_free/000848.html#more.

Simon, Ellen. "U.S. Supreme Court Garbage Decision Could Cost State Millions; Now Trash Can Travel Out of State." *Connecticut Law Tribune* (May 30, 2004).

Simon, Marlise. "Upheaval in the East: Pollution's Toll in Eastern Europe." *New York Times,* March 19, 1990.

Slack, R. J., J. R. Gronow, and N. Voulvoulis. "Hazardous Components of Household Waste." *Critical Reviews in Environmental Science and Technology* 34 (2004): 419–45.

Smith, Ted, David A. Sonnenfeld, and David Naguib Pellow. *Challenging the Chip: Labor Rights and Environmental Justice in the Global Electronics Industry.* Philadelphia: Temple University Press, 2006.

Solid Waste Digest. "Privatization Drivers." May 2002, 1–2.

Spar, Michael A., and Quian Cai. *2005 Virginia Population Estimates.* Charlottesville, Va.: University of Virginia, Weldon Cooper Center for Public Service, 2006.

Specter, Arlen. "Should States and Communities Be Allowed to Regulate Trash from Other States? Let States Regulate Interstate Waste." *Roll Call,* May 15, 2002. http://specter.senate.gov/public/index.cfm?FuseAction=NewsRoom .Articles &ContentRecord_id=0F37D844-AFA0-48BA-858D-211134700E3C.

Speth, James Gustave. *Red Sky at Morning: America and the Crisis of the Global Environment, a Citizen's Agenda for Action.* 2d ed. New Haven: Yale University Press, 2005.

Strasser, Susan. *Waste and Want: A Social History of Trash.* New York: Henry Holt, 1999.

Summers, Lawrence. "Let Them Eat Pollution." World Bank memo, reprinted in *The Economist,* February 8, 1992, 66.

Suro, Roberto. "Pollution-Weary Minorities Try Civil Rights Tack." *New York Times,* January 11, 1993.

Sze, Julie. *Noxious New York: The Racial Politics of Urban Health and Environmental Justice.* Cambridge: MIT Press, 2007.

Taylor, David. "Talking Trash: The Economic and Environmental Issues of Landfills." *Environmental Health Perspectives* 107, no. 8 (1999): A4049.

Thale, Christopher. "Waste Disposal." *Electronic Encyclopedia of Chicago.* Chicago: Chicago Historical Society, 2005. *http://www.encyclopedia.chicagohistory.org/ pages/1322.html.*

Thomas, Ken. "Michigan Members Seeking Action on Canadian Trash Measure." November 15, 2005. http://customwire.ap.org/dynamic/stories/M/MI_ CANADIAN_TRASH_MIOL-?SITE=MITRA&SECTION=HOME.

Thompson, Michael. *Rubbish Theory: The Creation and Destruction of Value.* Oxford: Oxford University Press, 1979.

Thomson, Vivian E., and Itaru Okuda. "Garbage In, Garbage Out: Virginia Is for Landfills." Paper presented at meeting of the American Political Science Association, Washington, D.C., September 2005. http://www.allacademic.com// metalp_mla_apa_research_citation/0/4/1/0/8/pages41085/p41085-1.php.

Thomson, Vivian E., and Mark H. White, "Garbage In, Garbage Out: Federalism and Solid Waste Management in the United States." Paper presented at "Quo Vadis Abfallwirtschaft—Liberal, communal oder kollegial?" conference, Augsburg, Germany, October 2003.

Thorneloe, Susan. "U.S. EPA's Field Test Programs to Update Data on Landfill Gas Emissions." Research Triangle Park, N.C.: EPA, 2003. http://*www.erefdn.org/ rpts_summary_ordrs/Landfillgas.pdf.*

Tierney, John. "The Big City: Trying to End Free Pickup of Trash." *New York Times,* April 16, 2002.

Toronto, City of. "Facts about Toronto's Trash." Toronto: City of Toronto, November 1, 2007. *http://www.toronto.ca/garbage/facts.htm*.

Ufner, Julie. "Supreme Court to Hear Garbage 'Flow Control' Case." National Association of Counties. Washington, D.C.: NACo, 2005. http://www.naco.org/Tem plate.cfm?Section=Publications&template=/ContentManagement/ContentDis play.cfm&ContentID=22195.

United Church of Christ. Commission for Racial Justice. *Toxic Waste and Race in the United States: A National Report on the Racial and Socioeconomic Characteristics of Communities with Hazardous Wastes Sites*. New York: Public Access, 1987. http://www.ucc.org/justice/witness/wfj041502.htm.

United Nations. Food and Agriculture Organization. *FAO Statistical Yearbook, 2005–2006*. Rome: FAO, 2006. http://www.fao.org/docrep/009/a0490m/a0490m00.htm.

Unnever, James D., Allan C. Kerkhoff, and Timothy J. Robinson. "District Variations in Educational Resources and Student Outcomes." *Economics of Education Review* 19 (2000): 245–59.

Ursery, Stephen. "Aiming High." *Waste Age*, November 1, 2008. http://wasteage .com/Recycling_And_Processing/aiming_high1108/.

———. "Kerry Vows to Ban Canadian Imports; Industry Skeptical." *Waste Age*, September 8, 2004.

U.S. Centers for Disease Control. "Children at Risk from Ozone Air Pollution—United States, 1991–1993." *Morbidity and Mortality Weekly Report* 44, no. 16 (April 28, 1995): 309–12. http://www.cdc.gov/mmwR/preview/mmwrhtml/00036902.htm#00001077.htm.

———. "Update: Blood Lead Levels—United States, 1991–1994." *Morbidity and Mortality Weekly Report* 46, no. 7 (February 21, 1997): 141–46.

U.S. Congress. *Congressional Record*. 108th Cong., 1st sess., 2003. Vol. 149.

U.S. Congress. House of Representatives. *International Solid Waste Importation and Management Act of 2006*. HR 2491, 109th Cong., 2d sess. http://thomas.loc .gov/cgi-bin/bdquery/z?d109:HR02491:@@@L&summ2=m&.

———. *Solid Waste Interstate Transportation Act of 2007*. HR 274, 110th Cong., 1st sess.http://thomas.loc.gov/cgi-bin/bdquery/D?d110:1:./temp/7Ebd5TQ3: @@@L&summ2=m&|/bss/110search.html|.

———. *State Waste Empowerment and Enforcement Provision Act of 2007*. HR 70, 110th Cong., 1st sess. http://thomas.loc.gov/cgi-bin/bdquery/D?d110:1:./temp/ 7Ebda6Z4:@@@L&summ2=m&|/bss/110search.html|.

———. *Taxpayer Relief through Municipal Waste Control Act of 1999*. HR 1270, 106th Cong., 1st sess. http://thomas.loc.gov/cgi-bin/bdquery/z?d106:HR01270: @@@D&summ2=m&.

———. Committee on Energy and Commerce. *Hearing before the Subcommittee on Environment and Hazardous Materials*. 108th Cong., 1st sess., July 23, 2003. http://energycommerce.house.gov/108/action/ 108-33.pdf.

U.S. Congress. Senate. *Solid Waste Interstate Transportation and Local Authority Act of 1999*. S 663, 106th Cong., 1st sess. http://thomas.loc.gov/cgi-bin/bdquery/ z?d106:SN00663:@@@D&summ2=m&.

———. Committee on Environment and Public Works. *Interstate Waste and Flow Control: Hearing before the Committee on Environment and Public Works.* 107th Cong., 2d sess., March 20, 2002. *http://frwebgate.access.gpo.gov/cgi-bin/getdoc .cgi?dbname=107_senate_hearings&docid=f:83690.wais.*

———. Committee on Environment and Public Works. *Transportation and Flow Control of Solid Waste: Hearing before the Committee on Environment and Public Works.* 105th Cong., 1st sess., March 18, 1997. Washington, D.C.: Government Printing Office, 1997.

U.S. Congressional Research Service. *Interstate Shipment of Municipal Solid Waste: 2004 Update.* Washington, D.C.: Congressional Research Service, 2004. http:// wastec.isproductions.net/webmodules/webarticles/articlefiles/430-CRS%2004%20Waste%20Numbers.pdf.

———. *Interstate Shipment of Municipal Solid Waste: 2007 Update.* Washington, D.C.: Congressional Research Service, 2007. http://www.ncseonline.org/NLE/ CRSreports/07Jul/RL34043.pdf.

———. *Interstate Trash Transport: Legislative Issues.* Issue brief for Congress by James E. McCarthy, 1999. http://www.cnie.org/nle/waste-29.cfm.

———. *Managing Electronic Waste: An Analysis of State E-Waste Legislation.* Report for Congress by Linda Luther, environmental policy analyst, updated February 6, 2008. http://ncseonline.org/NLE/CRSreports/08Mar/RL34147.pdf.

———. *Solid Waste Issues in the 106th Congress.* April 27, 2000. http://ncseonline.org/ NLE/CRS/abstract.cfm?NLEid=831.

U.S. Department of Agriculture. Economic Research Service. *Average Daily Per Capita Calories from the U.S. Food Availability, Adjusted for Spoilage and Other Waste.* Washington, D.C.: ERS, 2008. http://www.ers.usda.gov/Data/FoodCon sumption/FoodGuideIndex.htm#calories.

———. Economic Research Service. *International Macroeconomic Data Set: Real GDP (2000 Dollars) Historical.* Washington, D.C.: ERS, December 19, 2007. http:// www.ers.usda.gov/Data/macroeconomics/.

U.S. Department of Commerce. Bureau of Economic Analysis. "Consumer Expenditures in 2002." Washington, D.C.: Bureau of Economic Analysis, 2004. http://www.bls.gov/cex/csxann02.pdf.

———. Bureau of Economic Analysis. "Current Dollar and 'Real' Gross Domestic Product, 1929 to 2006." http://www.bea.gov/national/xls/gdplev.xls.

———. Bureau of Economic Analysis. "National Income and Product Accounts Tables: Table 2.1, Personal Income and Its Disposition." August 4, 2005. http:// www.bea.gov/bea/dn/nipaweb/TableView.asp#Mid.

———. Census Bureau. "Population, Housing Units, Area Measurements, and Density: 1790 to 1990." Washington, D.C.: U.S. Census Bureau, 2008. *http://www .census.gov/population/censusdata/table.2.pdf.*

———. Census Bureau. "Population Profile of the United States: 1995." Washington, D.C.: U.S. Census Bureau, 1995. http://www.census.gov/population/ www/pop-profile/toc.html.

———. Census Bureau. "USA Quick Facts." Washington, D.C.: U.S. Census Bureau, 2008. http://quickfacts.census.gov/qfd/states/00000.html.

———. Census Bureau. "Your Gateway to Census 2000." Washington, D.C.: U.S. Census Bureau, 2008. http://www.census.gov/main/www/cen2000.html.

U.S. Department of Health and Human Services. Agency for Toxic Substances and Disease Registry. "Landfill Gas Primer—An Overview for Environmental Health Professionals." 2001. http://www.atsdr.cdc.gov/HAC/landfill/html/intro.html.

U.S. Department of Labor. Bureau of Labor Statistics. "Consumer Expenditures in 2002." Washington, D.C.: Bureau of Labor Statistics, 2004. http://www.bls .gov/cex/csxann02.pdf.

U.S. Department of Transportation. Bureau of Transportation Statistics. "Virginia Transportation Profile—2000." Washington, D.C.: Bureau of Transportation, 2002. http://www.bts.gov/publications/state_transportation_profiles/virgin ia/pdf/entire.pdf.

U.S. Environmental Protection Agency. "FY 2008: EPA Budget in Brief." Washington, D.C.: EPA, 2008. *http://www.epa.gov/ocfo/budget/2008/2008bib.pdf*.

———. Office of Air and Radiation. *Acid Rain and Related Programs: 2006 Progress Report*. Washington, D.C.: EPA, 2007.

———. Office of Air and Radiation. "Air Regulations for Municipal Waste Combustors." http://www.epa.gov/reg3artd/airregulations/ap22/combust3.htm.

———. Office of Air and Radiation. "Fact Sheet: Proposed Federal Implementation Plan for the Clean Air Interstate Rule and Proposed Response to Section 126 Petition from North Carolina." Washington, D.C.: EPA, 2005. *http://www.epa.gov/ cair/fs20050801.html*.

———. Office of Solid Waste. "Assessment of OSW's 35 Percent Municipal Solid Waste National GPRA Goal for 2005." Exploratory study by Mark Eads, OSW analyst. Washington, D.C.: EPA, 2003.

———. Office of Solid Waste. "Characterization of Building-Related Construction and Demolition Debris in the United States." Washington, D.C.: EPA, 1995.

———. Office of Solid Waste. "Characterization of Municipal Solid Waste in the United States: 1996 Update." Washington, D.C.: EPA, 1997. http://www.epa .gov/epawaste/nonhaz/municipal/pubs/msw96rpt.pdf.

———. Office of Solid Waste. "Closure and Post-Closure Requirements for Municipal Solid Waste Landfills (MSWLFs)." Washington, D.C.: EPA, 2008. http:// www.epa.gov/osw/nonhaz/municipal/landfill/financial/mswclose.htm.

———. Office of Solid Waste. "Kim-Stan Landfill, Selma, Virginia." Washington, D.C.: EPA, 2007. *http:// www.epa.gov/superfund/accomp/factsheets05/kimstan.htm*.

———. Office of Solid Waste. "Management of Electronic Wastes in the United States." Washington, D.C.: EPA, 2007. http://www.epa.gov/e-Cycling/docs/ fact11-07.pdf.

———. Office of Solid Waste. "Materials Generated in the Municipal Waste Stream, 1960 to 2006." Washington, D.C.: EPA, 2007. http://www.epa.gov/osw/non haz/municipal/pubs/06data.pdf.

———. Office of Solid Waste. "Methane: Sources and Emissions." Washington, D.C.: EPA, 2005. http://*www.epa.gov/methane/sources.html*.

———. Office of Solid Waste. "MSW Programs." Washington, D.C.: EPA, 2008. *http://www.epa.gov/msw/programs.htm*.

———. Office of Solid Waste. *"Municipal Solid Waste Generation, Recycling, and Disposal in the United States: Facts and Figures for 2006."* Washington, D.C.: EPA, 2007. http://www.epa.gov/epawaste/nonhaz/municipal/pubs/msw06.pdf.

———. Office of Solid Waste. "Municipal Solid Waste in the United States: 2007 Facts and Figures." Washington, D.C.: EPA, 2008. http://www.epa.gov/epawaste/nonhaz/municipal/pubs/msw07-rpt.pdf.

———. Office of Solid Waste. "Recycling Is Working in the United States." Washington, D.C.: EPA, 2002. http://www.epa.gov/epawaste/conserve/rrr/pubs/rei-fs.pdf.

U.S. General Accounting Office. "Hazardous and Non-Hazardous Waste: Demographics of People Living Near Waste Facilities." Washington, D.C.: GAO, 1995.

———. "Siting of Hazardous Waste Landfills and Their Correlation with Racial and Economic Status of Surrounding Communities." GAO/RCED-83-168. Washington, D.C.: Government Printing Office, 1983.

U.S. Government Accountability Office. "Electronic Waste: Strengthening the Role of the Federal Government in Encouraging Recycling and Reuse." Washington, D.C.: GAO, 2005. http://www.gao.gov/new.items/d0647.pdf.

———. "Superfund: Funding and Reported Costs of Enforcement and Administration Activities." Washington, D.C.: GAO, 2005. http://www.gao.gov/products/GAO-08-841R.

Vandeputte, Anne. "Waste Management, Planning, and Results in Flanders." Public Waste Agency of Flanders. Mechelen, Belgium: OVAM, 2008. http://www.vmd.be/uploads/kroatie2008/20080327/01_OVAM_Zagreb_27_03_2008_bis.pdf.

Verchick, Robert R. M. "The Commerce Clause: Environmental Justice and the Interstate Garbage Wars." *Southern California Law Review* 70 (July 1997): 1239–1309.

Virginia Department of Environmental Quality. *Report on the Management of Municipal Solid Waste in the Commonwealth of Virginia: A Historical Review.* Richmond: Virginia DEQ, 1998. http://www.deq.state.va.us/waste/pdf/waste.pdf.

———. "Solid Waste Managed in Virginia during Calendar Year 2006." Richmond: Virginia DEQ, June 2007. http://www.deq.state.va.us/waste/pdf/swreport2006.pdf.

———. "Solid Waste Managed in Virginia during Calendar Year 2007." Richmond: Virginia DEQ, June 2008. http://www.deq.state.va.us/waste/pdf/swreport2007.pdf.

———. Solid Waste Management Facilities in Virginia. Richmond: Virginia DEQ, 2007. http://www.deq.state.va.us/export/sites/default/waste/pdf/swfrapro7.pdf.

Virginia General Assembly. Joint Legislative Audit and Review Commission. "Solid

Waste Management Facilities in Virginia: Impact on Minority Communities."
House Document no. 33. Richmond: Commonwealth of Virginia, 1995.

Voinovich, George. "Limits on Interstate Shipments of Solid Waste." Testimony before Senate Environment and Public Works Committee, March 20, 2002.
http://epw.senate.gov/107th/voi_032002.htm.

Wallgren, Christine. "City Wants BFI Landfill to Stay Shut: East Bridgewater Proposal Draws Fire." *Boston Globe,* October 14, 2004.

———. "Town Meeting Rejects BFI Plan." *Boston Globe,* November 11, 2004.

Weeks, Jennifer. "Take This Product Back and Recycle It!" *In Business,* November–December 2006, 12. *http://www.jgpress.com/inbusiness/archives/_free/001183.html.*

Weinberg, Philip. "Congress, the Courts, and Solid Waste Transport: Good Fences Don't Always Make Good Neighbors." *Environmental Law* 25 (1995): 57–72.

Whybrow, Peter C. *American Mania: When More Is Not Enough.* New York: W. W. Norton, 2005.

Williams, Bruce A., and Albert R. Matheny. *Democracy, Dialogue, and Environmental Disputes: The Contested Languages of Social Regulation.* New Haven: Yale University Press, 1995.

Xerox Corporation. *Revealing Our True Colors: 2006 Report on Global Citizenship.* Stamford, Conn.: Xerox Corp., 2006. http://www.xerox.com/Static_HTML/citizenshipreport/2006/citizenshipreport06.pdf.

Wines, Michael. "Malawi Is Burning, and Deforestation Erodes Economy." *New York Times,* November 1, 2005.

World Bank. *World Development Report 1992: Development and the Environment.* Washington, D.C.: World Bank, 1992.

Yardley, Jim. "China's Next Big Boom Could Be the Foul Air." *New York Times,* October 30, 2005.

Yoshida, F. "Case Studies of Environmental Politics in Japan." In *Environmental Policy in Japan,* ed. H. Imura and M. Schreurs. Cheltenham, UK: Edward Elgar, 2005.

Index

Municipal solid waste is abbreviated as MSW. Page numbers in italics refer to illustrations.